From Unequal to Unwanted:

Reforms Needed to Improve K–12 Public and Higher Education in America

By
James "Jim" Taylor

© 2018 James "Jim" Taylor

All Rights Reserved.

No part of this publication may be reproduced, stored in a retrieval system, or transmitted, in any form or by any means, electronic, mechanical, photocopying, recording, or otherwise, without the written permission of the author.

First published by Dog Ear Publishing
4011 Vincennes Rd
Indianapolis, IN 46268
www.dogearpublishing.net

ISBN: 978-1-4575-6114-6

This book is printed on acid-free paper.

Printed in the United States of America

Contents

Prologue v

Part I: America's Education System during the Twentieth Century ..1

Chapter 1:   Separate-and-Unequal During the Jim Crow Era 2

Chapter 2:   Desegregation During the Civil Rights Era 14

Chapter 3:   Equal-but-Unwanted in Higher Education During the Affirmative Action Era 25

Chapter 4:   Report Card for America's Education System During the Twentieth Century 44

Part II: **America's Education System during the Twenty-First Century** 61

Chapter 5:   Current Challenges in K–12 Public Education 62

Chapter 6:   Current Challenges in Higher Education 88

Part III: **Strategies for Twenty-First Century Reform in Education** 109

Chapter 7:   Higher Education—Reform Actions Needed 110

Chapter 8:   Public Education—Reform Actions Needed 125

Chapter 9:   C. A. Johnson Preparatory Academy: Reviving an All-Black Urban High School 154

Part IV: **Now What?** 183

Chapter 10:   Conclusion 184

Notes 192

Listing of Tables and Figures 214

Index 216

Acknowledgements

Throughout history women have played a pivotal role in the educational development of our nation's youth. I would like to acknowledge three special women who inspired me to pursue educational excellence at every level. First, there is my mother – the late Hattie Elizabeth Taylor. Despite the struggles she experienced with her attempts to receive an education during the oppressive Jim Crow Era, she remained steadfast and unmovable. My mother taught me the importance of developing my mind and believing that all things are possible through my faith and a good education.

The second woman who inspired me is Mrs. Thomasenia Benson, my mentor. Mrs. Benson shared her wisdom and 30-plus years of experience in education to help me develop my leadership skills. She taught me the importance of building positive relationships and leading by example. Mrs. Benson is an exceptional educator, and I am fortunate to have her as my friend and mentor.

Finally, there is Dr. Wandy W. Taylor, my beautiful wife. Wandy is an accomplished educator who has always been my "sounding board" and my confidant. Her passion for education is unapparelled, and she inspired me to write this book to help others understand the need for America to put forth a better effort to develop our greatest resource – our children. Mom, Thomasenia, and Wandy – thank you for everything!

Prologue

The late Hattie Elizabeth Evans Taylor, my mother, taught me at an early age that education was the one thing no one would be able take from me. As I reflect upon those words, I am reminded of the barriers I encountered during my pursuit of a quality public education in America. As a black male, many of those barriers appeared in the form of racial discrimination, disparate treatment, and low expectations from many of my teachers from elementary school through college. In this prologue, I will share a brief personal account of my educational experience across three decades within the context of three distinct eras that defined education for blacks in America during the twentieth century: 1) separate-and-unequal, 2) desegregation, and 3) equal-but-unwanted.

Elementary school. I began my career in public education in the early1950s at Carver Elementary, which was a *separate-and-unequal* school in the segregated Deep South. During that time of legal segregation, blacks attended what were described as substandard schools. All my teachers were black females who encouraged me and my classmates to work hard, be respectful, and strive for academic excellence. My parents reinforced and instilled those same values in me at home.

Despite the oppression of a racially segregated society in the early 1950s, I had a wonderful educational experience in elementary school. I received a strong foundation in basic academic skills, especially in reading, and the teachers nurtured my insatiable thirst for knowledge. Most importantly, I was in an environment where all children were treated fairly, and the teachers had high expectations for all students. I enjoyed being a young black male in my elementary school because I felt loved and respected.

Middle school. Things really changed in middle school. In 1960, my family moved to Augsburg, Germany, to join my father, a career noncommissioned officer in the United States Army. The schools overseas were integrated and operated by the U.S. Department of Defense Dependent Schools (DoDDS). When I entered my first classroom at Augsburg Middle School, I experienced a cold slap of culture shock. Both the teacher and overwhelming majority of the students were white. Julio Cruz, my light-skinned friend from Puerto Rico, and I were the only nonwhite students in my sixth-grade class.

I never had a black teacher during my three years of middle school in Germany. Unlike my teachers in elementary school, many of the white teachers in my integrated middle school overseas made me feel invisible and unwanted in their predominantly white classrooms. I was usually assigned to a seat near the back of the classroom, and I was often ignored whenever I raised my hand to participate in class discussions. Words of encouragement or praise were seldom cast in my direction. This was the first time I ever felt alienated in an educational setting.

By seventh grade, the sense of pride I felt in elementary school crept back into my psyche. I became more assertive and began to express concerns regarding the disparate treatment I was receiving. I openly challenged what I perceived as an unfair grading system, which made it exceedingly difficult for me to attain academic honors. Unfortunately, my teachers and the school's administrators viewed my assertiveness and willingness to voice my concerns as a form of insolence. This often resulted in them imposing disciplinary actions against me in the form of verbal reprimands and/or in-school suspensions.

High school. My high school years presented a study in contrasts. I completed my first two years of high school at Laughbon High in DuPont, Washington, which served the dependents of military personnel stationed at Fort Lewis. Although the student population was somewhat diverse (roughly 80% white; 20% nonwhite), the entire faculty and staff were white. For the most part, my experience at Laughbon High School was pleasant. Although the teachers appeared to respect my academic skills, I cannot remember any of them ever having an interest in assisting me with my overall development as a person. I truly believe some of the teachers wanted to give me some moral support, but they simply did not know how to nurture a young black male student.

In 1965, I experienced my second dose of culture shock in public education; however, the shock was rather warm, not cold. My father was transferred to Fort Jackson, South Carolina, and I enrolled at C. A. Johnson High (CAJ), a segregated school with an all-black student enrollment. Although all public-school systems in the state were segregated at that time, many of them were in the process of developing plans for *desegregation*. Eleven years earlier, the United States Supreme Court had issued a federal mandate requiring all states to end segregation "with all deliberate speed." Like most states in the Deep South, South Carolina's response to the mandate was far more deliberate than speedy.

At CAJ, I was taught by black teachers for the first time since fifth grade. Moreover, I was taught by my first black male teacher ever. Within a matter of days, my homeroom teacher, Mr. Earl Reuben, adopted me as his protégé. He became my first-ever male role model in public school. Under his mentorship, I thrived as a student and graduated from high school with high academic honors and received scholarship offers from several colleges.

College. In 1966, I was among the first wave of African American students to integrate the University of South Carolina (USC). While the state's public schools were struggling with desegregating their campuses, the colleges and universities were progressing with greater "deliberate speed." Nevertheless, the mid-60s were turbulent times and racism ran rampant on many college campuses, including mine. This marked my first experience in an educational setting that was undergoing a bona fide process of desegregation. Despite episodes of racism, stereotypes, low expectations, unfair grading, and feeling unwanted in many classrooms, I remained steadfast and graduated from USC in 1970.

From a legal standpoint, public schools in America have changed dramatically since I walked the hallowed halls of Carver Elementary in the 1950s and C. A. Johnson in the mid-1960s. Back then, schools operated in a *de jure* or legally segregated society. Although the schools serving black students were separated from those that served whites, they were not equal. The schools that served white students had better facilities, more resources, and up-to-date textbooks. And those blatant disparities were considered legal and permissible at that time.

Today, pursuant to federal statutes, all schools in America are supposed to be desegregated. Yet, students of color encounter many of the same roadblocks I faced across three decades of discrimination from the 1950s through the 1970s. Those roadblocks continue to include racial stereotypes, disparate treatment in discipline, and low expectations from teachers. The ever-increasing diversity in America during the twenty-first century has produced an educational system in which *de facto* discrimination is causing children of color to feel *equal-but-unwanted* in their schools.

If America is to continue to act as the leader of the free world, it is incumbent upon educators and policymakers to work together to develop the full potential of all children regardless of their race, creed, color, socioeconomic status, religion, or gender. An educational system where children of color endure real or perceived feelings of being "unwanted" is destined to fail. Any form of discrimination can debilitate the socio-emotional and educational development of our country's greatest resource—our children.

This book provides historical data to describe the challenges that students of color have faced—and continue to face—in America's education system. Throughout this book, the ethnic terms *blacks* and *African Americans* will be used interchangeably. It is my hope that this book will enlighten educators and pave the way for them to accept the strategies for reform and perspectives that are offered to address problems that are smothering our country's system of public and higher education.

PART I

AMERICA'S EDUCATION SYSTEM DURING THE TWENTIETH CENTURY

CHAPTER 1

Separate-and-Unequal During the Jim Crow Era

The Great Depression in America began on October 24, 1929, when the stock market crashed. Not so ironically, this infamous date was dubbed "Black Thursday." During the time of that global financial crisis, the unemployment rate stood at a staggering 25 percent. Throughout America, and especially in the Deep South, black citizens endured devastating poverty and significantly higher levels of unemployment when compared to their white counterparts' due to pervasive and systemic racism.

Under President Franklin D. Roosevelt, a "New Deal" was implemented that lifted the United States out of the great economic depression. President Roosevelt's New Deal is often summed up as the "Three Rs":

- *Relief* for the unemployed
- *Recovery* of the economy through federal spending
- *Reform* of capitalism through the creation of social welfare programs

Although the New Deal brought economic prosperity back to the United States in 1939, blacks continued to suffer harsh economic depression due to limited access to jobs as well as education suppression because of limited access to a different set of three Rs"—*reading*, *'riting* (writing), and *'rithmetic* (arithmetic).

As a society, America must be mindful of her cultural past before any substantive changes can be made to ensure that all children have equal access to a quality public education in the future. The ugliness of our nation's past is captured in the infamous Jim Crow system or culture that operated primarily in, but not limited to, the southern and border states between 1877 and the mid-1960s. The Jim Crow culture was steeped in the beliefs or rationalizations that whites were superior to blacks in all important ways, especially in the areas of intelligence, morality, and civilized behavior. Some tenets of the infamous, degrading, and oppressive Jim Crow system in America included etiquette norms such as the following:

1. A black male could not shake hands with a white male because it implied being socially equal.
2. A black male could not offer his hand or any other part of his body to a white woman because he risked being accused of rape.
3. A black male could never offer to light the cigarette of a white female because that gesture implied intimacy.
4. A black male could never comment on a white woman's appearance.
5. Blacks and whites were not supposed to eat together.
6. Blacks were not allowed to show public affection toward each other in public, especially kissing, because it offended whites.
7. Whites did not use courtesy titles of respect (e.g., Mr., Mrs., Sir, or Ma'am) when referring to blacks.
8. A black could never lay claim to, or overtly demonstrate, superior knowledge or intelligence.

Undoubtedly, black males were the primary targets of the evil Jim Crow system of overt racism, even though the passage of the 13th (abolished slavery), 14th (citizenship), and 15th (right to vote) Amendments to the Constitution had given blacks the same legal protections as whites. Unfortunately, the United States Supreme Court helped to weaken those protections through its ruling in the infamous *Plessy v Ferguson* case.

The Plessy case involved a challenge to a Jim Crow law that was known as the Separate Car Act, which was passed by Louisiana in 1890. Under that act, blacks and whites were required to have separate accommodations on railroad facilities. On June 7, 1892, Homer Plessy, a man of mixed-race, bought a first-class ticket and sat in the "whites only" section of a passenger train. When he was asked to vacate the seat, Plessy refused, was arrested, and subsequently charged with violating the Separate Car Act.

In 1896, the Supreme Court upheld the Louisiana law and ruled that racially separate facilities, if equal, did not violate the Constitution. This ruling represented the legitimization of two societies in America. One society was white and advantaged, the other was black and despised and disadvantaged. The Court said segregation was not discrimination. In reality, blacks never experienced anything "equal" during the Jim Crow era. In fact, in Jim Crow America, the society for black Americans was *separate-and-unequal.*

Racist School Literature

Perhaps the greatest adverse impact of the Jim Crow doctrine of racial segregation occurred in America's public education system. Through a system of *de jure* racism, white children and white educators were deceived into believing that blacks, especially males, were intellectually inferior. A great deal of this deception was spread in racist children's books, which was the primary form of "social media" during that era.

In the late nineteenth century, Joel Chandler Harris used this social media of that time to taint the image of black males. Harris published a series of seven books that all featured Uncle Remus, a fictional former slave, who used a storytelling approach with animal characters to narrate folktales to children around him. The stories were told in what is known as an *eye dialect*, which is a technique whereby misspellings (e.g., *wuz* for *was*, *wimmin* for women, *enuff* for *enough*) are used to make the speaker appear boorish and uneducated. Through this technique, Uncle Remus was projected as a pleasant but ignorant old black man who did not pose an intellectual threat to white children.

Brer Rabbit (Brother Rabbit) is the main character in Uncle Remis' stories. He is a likeable character who often played tricks on two other characters: Brer Fox and Brer Bear. In one of the most famous tales, *The Wonderful Tar-Baby Story*, Brer Fox mixed some tar and turpentine and sculpted it into the figure of a little black boy. When Brer Rabbit comes along, he addresses the tar-baby cordially but receives no response. Brer Rabbit becomes offended by what he perceives as bad manners and proceeds to punch the tar-baby.

The message in this tale is undeniable. Black males (or tar-babies) during the Jim Crow era were expected to be subservient, obedient, and submissive. When black males either wittingly or unwittingly failed to display good manners, they often received some sort of brutal punishment, which could range from beatings to lynching.

Another inauspicious "rabbit" that appeared in children's literature during the Jim Crow era was the infamous George Washington Rabbit. This fictional little black boy lived in a dilapidated shack with his "mammy" (mother) on the edge of a cotton field in the Deep South, and he frequently ran errands for his "granny" (grandmother). The story revolved around George Washington Rabbit's inability to adequately perform the simplest tasks for his granny. He completely fulfilled the negative stereotype of a dimwitted and unattractive little black school-aged boy in rural America.

While the images of black males were being shaped in elementary schools in Jim Crow America through characters like tar-babies, Uncle Remus, and George Washington Rabbit, students in secondary schools received more advanced lessons in the stereotypes of black males by reading literary books like Mark Twain's *The Adventures of Huckleberry Finn*. One of the main characters in this book is Jim, a runaway slave who embodied many of the negative stereotypes of blacks during that period, such as being overly superstitious and submissive to whites. In addition to being exposed to negative stereotypes of blacks, the readers became more aware of the then-proper way to address them. In his book, Mark Twain uses the word "nigger" more than 200 times to reference blacks. This epithet was, and remains, the principal term in the lexicon of white racism that is used to stereotype blacks as lazy, stupid, inferior, and worthless.

Self-Esteem Among Black Children

Not surprisingly, systemic stereotyping and racism during the Jim Crow era had a debilitating impact on the self-esteem and self-perception of many black children in America. Kenneth and Mamie Clark conducted a classic study in 1939 to illustrate this impact. In their study, the Clarks showed 250 black children (ages two to seven) two sets of dolls that were identical except for their skin and hair color. Then the children were asked to select a doll according to each of the following specific verbal requests:

- Show me the doll that you would like to play with.
- Show me the doll that that is a nice doll.
- Show me the doll that looks bad.
- Show me the doll that looks like a white child.
- Show me the doll that looks like a colored child.
- Show me the doll that looks like a Negro child.
- Show me the doll that looks like you.

The Clarks found that most of the children overwhelmingly selected the white doll as the nice doll and the one they wanted to play with. Only 61 percent of the children selected the black doll (their own race) when asked to "give me the doll that looks like you." Some of the children refused to pick either doll or simply started crying and ran away. The study showed that, in Jim Crow America, the stereotyping of black people as bad and white people as nice began as early as age four.

The doll study was not immune to criticism. Many researchers questioned the methodology that was used as well as the validity of the study. However, most of us can agree that two distinct societies and educational systems existed in the Deep South during the time when the Clarks conducted their study. While the societies were separate, they were by no means equal. This begs the question: What were schools like for black children in Jim Crow America?

Substandard Schooling

At the beginning of the twentieth century, the basic curriculum in black primary schools reflected the limited jobs that were available to African Americans. During the early 1900s, most blacks lived in the Deep South and over half were employed as sharecroppers on white-owned farms. Typically, a white landowner saw little value in educating black children because they believed education would have no positive impact on their ability to pick cotton or wash laundry. Besides, in the minds of many white landowners, an education would only serve to encourage black children to seek higher wages and employment elsewhere. Therefore, it was socially and economically advantageous for most white landowners to keep black children uninformed and uneducated.

Despite massive economic and social obstacles in the 1930s, many black children were hungry for an education. More than three million school-age black American children lived in the 17 Jim Crow states that operated segregated schools. Those states stretched from Texas to Delaware, and their local school boards typically spent three times as much on each white student as they did on blacks. For example, in 1930, Georgia spent $32 on each white child and just $7 on those that were black. In South Carolina, the disparity was even greater, with $53 spent for each white child and $5 for each black child.

Interest in the plight of black children in the Deep South began to rise in the late 1930s. Reports of systemic violations of child labor and compulsory education laws prompted key governmental agencies to launch investigations. One agency, the American Council on Education, sent a team of investigators to the Deep South to assess the legally segregated, state-supported public schools for black children. The investigative report compiled by the team who visited the black grade school in Dine Hollow, Alabama, reflected the widespread findings across the 17 Jim Crow states (also known as the "Black Belt"). The investigators reported the following:

> A typical rural Negro school is at Dine Hollow. It is in a dilapidated building, once whitewashed, standing in a rocky field unfit for cultivation. Dust-covered weeds spread a carpet all around, except for an uneven, bare area on one side that looks like a ball field. Behind the school is a small building with a broken, sagging door. As we

approach, a nervous, middle-aged woman comes to the door of the school. She greets us in a discouraged voice marked by a speech impediment. Escorted inside, we observe that the broken benches are crowded to three times their normal capacity. Only a few battered books are in sight, and we look in vain for maps or charts. We learn that four grades are assembled here. The weary teacher agrees to permit us to remain while she proceeds with the instruction. She goes to the blackboard and writes an assignment for the first two grades to do while she conducts spelling and word drills for the third and fourth grades. This is the assignment:

Write your name ten times.

Draw an dog, an cat, an rat, an boot.

The scenario described at Dine Hollow is a sad reminder of the deplorable separate-and-unequal conditions that prevailed for black Americans in education during the Jim Crow era. Most teachers in black schools like the one at Dine Hollow did not have the benefit of decent books or a written curriculum. Typically, no real teaching and learning occurred in the classroom; the children were simply given "busy work" to keep them occupied. The so-called education for most black children did not extend beyond the rudiments of literacy and figuring. One can only imagine the achievement gap that existed between children in the all-black school in Dine Hollow and their counterparts in the neighboring all-white schools.

Sadly, only a small number of black children who finished grade school in the 1930s had the opportunity to attend high school. This was due in large part to the fact that very few states in the so-called Black Belt had black high schools that were accredited for four-year study. A report on secondary education for blacks in 1933 showed that, collectively, the states of Florida, Louisiana, Mississippi, and South Carolina had a grand total of only 16 black high schools that were accredited for four-year study. In addition to having teachers with minimal training, very few of the black high schools offered science courses, foreign languages, music, or art. Indeed, the schooling for black children was substandard.

Violent Reaction to Black Prosperity

Despite the pervasive economic depression and education suppression in Jim Crow America, there were occasions when blacks overcame staggering odds to achieve success. In the early 1900s, many African Americans migrated from the hardships of the Black Belt hoping to seek prosperity elsewhere. Tulsa, Oklahoma, had experienced a major oil boom during that time. Thousands of blacks flocked to Tulsa to pursue their dream of having better educational and economic opportunities.

Although Jim Crow laws were enforced and caused segregation in Tulsa, many African Americans still migrated to the region and settled in the northern section of the town in an area known as the Greenwood District. In 1906, under the leadership of a black landowner named O. W. Gurley, the township's black residents adopted an entrepreneurial focus. By 1921, the Greenwood District experienced a phenomenal boom. There were over 11,000 residents in the district, and hundreds of prosperous black-owned businesses were established that were patronized by both black and white consumers. This epicenter for black-owned businesses became known as the "Black Wall Street."

The black community in Tulsa realized the importance of education to sustain their cultural and economic success. Therefore, their primary objective was to educate every child. When the average black male student went to school on Black Wall Street, he wore a suit and tie because of the morals and respect they were taught at a young age. Physicians in that community owned a medical school, and they actively recruited high-performing students to train as physicians.

Despite the huge educational and economic success of the Black Wall Street, which was one of the most affluent all-black communities in America, Jim Crow destroyed it. At that time, one of the quickest ways to raise the ire and bigotry of white men in Jim Crow America was to fabricate an allegation of a black male showing "disrespect" toward a white woman. That ire-raising scenario became a reality on May 30, 1921, when all hell broke loose shortly after a white woman filed a false allegation against a nineteen-year-old black male in Tulsa named Dick Rowland.

On June 1, 1921, a mob of angry Ku Klux Klan–influenced white men stormed into the Black Wall Street community armed with firearms provided by local law enforcement officers. They ransacked and set businesses afire; indiscriminately shot and killed unarmed black men, women, and children; and used World War I airplanes to fire rifles and drop fire bombs on the black community. At the end of twenty-four hours of carnage, approximately 3,000 blacks were dead and over 600 successful businesses destroyed.

There is no moral to the story of Black Wall Street; there is only immorality. In Jim Crow America, the "all men are created equal" proviso in the Declaration of Independence only applied to whites. Blacks were expected to adopt a slave mentality of inferiority and submissiveness. Moreover, black children were not supposed to reap the benefits of a free, high-quality public education and pursue professional careers in law and medicine. The Black Wall Street community dared to do otherwise and paid the ultimate price for doing so.

Ideology of Two Black Scholars

During the Jim Crow era of institutional segregation and racism, two key black scholars offered divergent views regarding education. Booker T. Washington, who was the most influential black man in America during that era, postulated the most dominant educational ideology for blacks. He urged blacks to accept racial subordination as an unavoidable circumstance at that time, and he encouraged them to elevate themselves through hard work and economic gain. Washington insisted that an industrial education would enable black Americans to win the respect of whites and enable them to escape the bondage of sharecropping and debt.

W. E. B. Du Bois, the first black man to earn a doctoral degree at Harvard, argued against the principles that were espoused by Booker T. Washington. Du Bois argued that blacks should never entertain the idea of accepting biological white superiority and the notion that their best pathway to a meaningful education was through the industrial arts. Instead, he urged blacks to pursue an education in the liberal arts to broaden their intellectual acumen. DuBois was also a vocal supporter of women's rights, and he co-founded the National Association for the Advancement of Colored People in 1909.

Despite their philosophical differences, both Washington and Du Bois wanted the same thing for blacks—first class citizenship. They agreed that education was the pathway to earning respect and prosperity in a white-dominated society. Many African American scholars and historians consider Washington and Du Bois the pioneer civil rights leaders in the twentieth century.

Chapter Summary

The Jim Crow era marked an extremely difficult period for black children in America. The seeds of economic depression, coupled with being denied access to a free public education while living in an oppressive society, sprouted weeds of despair, helplessness, and hopelessness. Black children, especially boys, were stereotyped as unattractive buffoons in children's literature books, and they lived in an ugly society that had little expectation that they would ever bloom into beautiful flowers of success. On average, African American children in the so-called Black Belt received roughly 75 days of schooling in dilapidated facilities each year as compared to the180 days their white counterparts experienced in more stimulating educational settings.

Under the pervasive Jim Crow doctrine in America from the late 1880s through circa 1950, black children were expected to accept their status as being submissive and inferior to whites. The doll study conducted by the Clarks in 1939 provided evidence that the openly racist society in America had, indeed, negatively impacted the self-concept of many black children. They perceived themselves as being unattractive, inferior, and undesirable; just what Jim Crow wanted.

Despite the clouds of despair and racism that existed during the Jim Crow era, blacks continued to crave knowledge and desired to reap the benefits of a good public education. Black scholars at that time had two contrasting points of view regarding education. Booker T. Washington believed blacks should pursue an education in farming or the industrial arts. He said this would earn the respect of whites and enable blacks the opportunity to advance in society.

W. E. B. Du Bois rejected Washington's point of view and argued that it would perpetuate the white oppression of blacks. Du Bois believed that blacks should pursue an education in the liberal arts, because it would prepare them to interact with whites at a higher intellectual level. In short, Washington wanted blacks to pursue an education to develop their hands, while Du Bois wanted them to pursue an education to develop their minds.

After the civil war, the general philosophy that emerged in the Deep South was that if African Americans were kept ill-educated they would "remain in their place" in society. An educated "boy" could become a danger. The ideology of most white leaders and policymakers during the Jim Crow era was that a poor education guaranteed a poor lifestyle for African Americans. A system of separate-and-unequal schools advanced that ideology for most of the twentieth century.

CHAPTER 2

Desegregation During the Civil Rights Era

Despite the United States Supreme Court's ruling in *Plessy* and similar cases, many people continued to press for the abolition of Jim Crow and other racially discriminatory laws. Organizations and agencies understood that any fight to repeal those race-based laws had to occur in the arena of a federal court. One organization that fought for racial equality was the National Association for the Advancement of Colored People (NAACP). Under the leadership of Thurgood Marshall, members of the NAACP's Legal Defense and Education Fund devised a strategy to attack Jim Crow laws at arguably their weakest point, which was in the field of education.

While Thurgood Marshall was leading the charge for equal education for blacks, the Reverend Dr. Martin Luther King, Jr. emerged as the leader for civil rights reform. Both men took their fight to Washington, D.C. Thurgood Marshall took his fight to the Supreme Court, and Dr. King appealed to the conscience of the president of the United States. The legal battle for civil rights reform began in 1950 when several pivotal education-related cases were argued in federal courts to dispute racial segregation in both public and higher education.

The year 1954 marked America's transition from a legal Jim Crow system of segregated schools (separate-and-unequal) to a *de facto* system of segregated schools because states in the Deep South refused to adhere to the Supreme Court's order to desegregate. A major focus of the Civil Rights era was to gain real equality for black children in America's education system. The struggles that were involved with legally obtaining and enforcing the desegregation of the institutions of public and higher education in the United States are chronicled in the next subsections of this chapter.

Pivotal Supreme Court Cases

The case of *Sweatt v Painter (1950)* was one of the NAACP's first attacks on racial discrimination in higher education. In 1946, a black man named Heman Sweatt applied for admission into the University of Texas' law school. At that time, the university only had an all-white law school. Therefore, in hopes that it would not have to admit Sweatt into the all-white law school, the university hastily created an underfunded "black" law school on its campus to accommodate black applicants. In response to the university's actions, Sweatt retained the services of Thurgood Marshall and the NAACP's Legal Defense and Education Fund and sued to be admitted into the University's all-white law school.

The Sweatt case reached the United States Supreme Court in 1950 and the justices unanimously agreed with the plaintiff. In its decision, the nation's highest court cited the blatant inequalities between the university's law school for whites vis-à-vis the hastily created law school for blacks. More specifically, the so-called black law school was "separate" but "not equal." Accordingly, the Court found the only appropriate remedy for this situation was to admit Heman Sweatt into the University of Texas's law school.

The case of *McLaurin v Oklahoma Board of Regents* (1950) also involved higher education. Despite having admitted George McLaurin, a black male, into its doctoral program in 1949, the University of Oklahoma required him to sit apart from the rest of the class and eat at a separate time and table from white students. McLaurin sued the university, asserting their actions were discriminatory and had a debilitating impact on his academic pursuits. Thurgood Marshall and the NAACP Legal Defense and Education Fund argued his case.

As expected, the case reached the Supreme Court. Ironically, the Court's opinion was rendered on the same day as its decision in the Sweatt case. The Court ruled that the university's actions regarding McLaurin were discriminatory and impeded his ability to learn. The school was ordered to immediately cease and desist with its discriminatory activity.

Brown v Board of Education (1954) is the name given to five separate cases that were heard by the Supreme Court regarding the issue of segregation in public schools. Those cases were *Brown v Board of Education of Topeka (KS); Boiling v Sharpe (DC); Briggs v Elliot (SC); Davis v Board of Education of Prince Edward County (VA);* and *Gebhart v Ethel (DE).* While the facts of each case were different, the main issue in each was the constitutionality of state-sponsored segregation in public schools. Marshall personally argued the case before the Supreme Court and raised a variety of legal issues.

The most common argument Marshall posed to the Court was that separate school systems for blacks and whites were inherently unequal and, consequently, violated the "equal protection clause" of the 14th Amendment of the U.S. Constitution. He cited sociological data such as the research conducted by Kenneth Clark in 1939 to support his argument that segregated school systems tended to make African American children feel inferior to white children. Marshall reasoned that such a system should not be legally permissible.

On May 14, 1954, the Supreme Court delivered what has been acknowledged as one of the greatest decisions of the twentieth century. The Court ruled unanimously (9-0) that racial segregation of children in public schools violated the Equal Protection Clause of the 14th Amendment. Essentially, the Court concluded that in the field of public education, the doctrine of "separate but equal" has no place in America's society, because separate educational facilities are inherently unequal and discriminatory.

Resistance to "Brown" in Public Education

When the Supreme Court rendered its landmark decision in the 1954 *Brown* case, the justices expected opposition—especially in the southern states. Therefore, rather than giving immediate direction regarding implementation of the new federal law, the Court asked the attorney generals for all states with laws permitting public school segregation to submit action plans as to how they would proceed with desegregation. By 1955, public schools in many southern counties in America remained segregated (separate-and-unequal). This prompted the Court to issue a mandate urging states to proceed with "all deliberate speed" to desegregate their public schools.

Unfortunately, there was far more deliberation than speed. A decade after the *Brown* decision, only a small percentage of black children in the Deep South attended schools with white children. Opposition to the *Brown* decision was intense in some places. Governors stood defiantly in schoolhouse doors and angry whites terrorized black children. In 1957, Arkansas Governor Orval Faubus – a staunch segregationist – ordered 100 armed-National Guard troops to encircle Little Rock's Central High School to prevent nine black students from attending. Desegregation was only achieved after a powerful show of force by federal troops.

Although the nine black students were granted permission to enroll and attend Central High, they were often victims of verbal and physical assaults. One of the nine, Melba Patillo, had acid thrown in her eyes, and another black girl was pushed down a flight of stairs. The three male students were subjected to more conventional physical assaults. This abuse occurred even though federal troops remained on the campus throughout the school year.

In defiance of the federal government, Governor Faubus continued to fight the school board's plan for desegregation. In September 1958, he ordered all-white high schools in Little Rock to close rather than permit integration. Many of Little Rock's white students lost a year of education because of the governor's racial bigotry and legal fight over desegregation. In 1959, a federal court struck down Faubus's school-closing law.

In one of the five school districts in the 1954 school desegregation cases (viz., Prince Edward, Virginia), county officials decided to close public schools altogether rather than integrate. Tuition benefits were provided to children to attend private schools; however, the only private schools in that county had white-only admission policies. In 1964, the Supreme Court intervened and ruled that Prince Edward's closing of the public-school system violated equal protection. Thus, the county was ordered to reopen all its public schools.

Violent resistance to integration was not restricted to high school settings in the Deep South. Despite repeated attempts in federal court to stall the desegregation process, the state of Louisiana eventually adhered to the *Brown* decision and accepted school desegregation as the nation's rule of law. In 1960, the NAACP informed Abon and Lucille Bridges that their daughter – Ruby Bridges – would be the first black child to attend the all-white William Frantz Elementary School in New Orleans, which was only a few blocks from her house.

On the morning of November 14, 1960, escorted by four white court-appointed federal marshals to protect her, six-year-old Ruby Bridges became the first black child to attend an all-white elementary school in the

South. The image of this innocent little black girl being escorted to school by four large white men inspired Norman Rockwell to create the painting, *The Problem We Must All Live With*. This painting subsequently appeared on the cover of *Look* magazine in 1964.

Despite the presence of four federal marshals, Ruby was subjected to many episodes of deliberate racism from members of the Frantz School community. On her second day of school, a woman threatened to poison Ruby, and on another occasion, she was antagonized by a woman displaying a black doll in a wooden coffin. There was also resistance from adults inside the school. For a while it looked as if Ruby would have to withdraw from school because no teacher would teach her. Fortunately, a new teacher – Mrs. Barbara Henry from Boston – accepted Ruby with open arms and agreed to teach her.

Ruby became the sole student in Mrs. Henry's class because parents either withdrew or threatened to withdraw their children from her class. For the entire school year, Mrs. Henry and Ruby sat side-by-side at two desks completing assignments. Mrs. Henry was very nurturing and supportive of Ruby, and she helped the six-year-old cope with some of the social and emotional stress she experienced in the school's hostile environment.

Things took a dramatic shift for Ruby during her second year at Frantz School. Most noticeably, Mrs. Henry was no longer there. Her contract was not renewed, so Mrs. Henry and her husband returned to Boston. In addition, there were no more federal marshals; Ruby walked to school every day by herself. There were other students in her second-grade class and enrollment at the school started to increase again. It seemed as if the Frantz community wanted to put the experience of the previous school year behind them. Some things, however, cannot be swept under a rug and simply disappear. Memorialized in Rockwell's painting, Ruby's story is etched in America's history of public education for upcoming generations to review.

A possible silver lining in the Ruby Bridges's story lies in its alignment with a popular education axiom—good teachers matter! As an adult, Ruby acknowledged the role her nurturing teacher, Mrs. Henry, played on her ability to cope with the stress and turmoil she experienced during her first year at Frantz Elementary School. In 1996, Ruby and Mrs. Henry were reunited on an episode of the *Oprah Winfrey Show*. That reunion touched the hearts of millions of viewers and served as a reminder of the vitriol and hatred that was directed at an innocent six-year-old black girl who simply wanted to attend the school near her home in 1960.

Resistance to "Brown" in Higher Education

On February 27, 2017, U. S. Secretary of Education Betsy DeVos released the following official statement shortly after meeting with several presidents of historically black colleges and universities (HBCUs): "These are real pioneers when it comes to school choice. HBCUs are living proof that when more options are provided to students, they are afforded greater access and greater quality. Their success has shown that more options help students flourish."

To imply that HBCUs were designed in the spirit of "school choice" is like arguing that black people left Africa because they were tired of the freezing weather; hence, their great migration to America ensued. HBCUs were not founded to offer a "choice" option to black students—it was their only choice in a segregated society that openly discriminated against them. When African American students attempted to exercise a nonexistent "choice" option to enroll in an undergraduate program at an all-white college in the *Brown* era, they were met with fierce resistance.

In 1953, more than 75,000 students were enrolled in undergraduate programs and 3,200 in graduate programs at HBCUs. As stipulated in two Supreme Court decisions that were mentioned earlier (i.e., *McLaurin v Oklahoma Board of Regents,* [1950]; *Sweatt v Painter* [1950]), black students were typically admitted to graduate and professional schools if their program of study was not available at an HBCU. Therefore, desegregation in higher education began at the post-baccalaureate level.

In the summer of 1959, two black students – Hamilton Holmes and Charlayne Hunter – applied for admission to the University of Georgia (UGA). However, they were denied enrollment because the dormitories, allegedly, were filled to capacity. The two students renewed their applications each semester thereafter with the same results. Tensions mounted, and a legal battle ensued.

In the wake of an impending lawsuit from the NAACP, the Board of Regents hastily approved a variety of new and controversial admission requirements that were designed to keep colleges and universities in Georgia segregated. Under their new guidelines, student-applicants were required to complete a battery of psychometric instruments as part of the admissions process. The scoring for these tests was highly subjective and the results could easily be manipulated to achieve a desired outcome.

In addition, the Georgia General Assembly passed a bill that imposed age limits on applicants applying for admission to an all-white public college or university. Students applying for undergraduate school had to be younger than 21, and those applying for graduate or professional school had to be younger than 25. The new guidelines effectively disqualified Holmes and Hunter.

The NAACP presented the case against the Board of Regents in federal court. On January 6, 1961, U.S. District Court Judge William Bootie ordered the university to admit Holmes and Hunter. The school's administration adhered to the judge's ruling, thereby ending 160 years of segregation at the University of Georgia. Other public and private colleges desegregated their institutions in the years that followed.

Although Holmes and Hunter would later recall having experienced a great deal of unpleasantness during their time at UGA, neither felt as if they ever were in physical danger while on campus. The same cannot be said regarding the desegregation of the University of Mississippi. That university's first black student was subjected to harsh racism and constant physical threats to his life.

From 1960 to 1962, James Meredith studied at the all-black Jackson State College, and, during that time, he applied repeatedly to attend the University of Mississippi (Ole Miss) without success. Meredith, a mature man who had served nine years in the United States Air Force, contacted the NAACP to file a lawsuit against the university on his behalf. The case eventually reached the Supreme Court, which ruled in his favor in September 1962.

The governor of Mississippi, Ross Barnett, and other state officials provoked a constitutional crisis with a blatant attempt to defy the court's decision. When Meredith arrived at the school's campus in Oxford, Mississippi, under the protection of federal forces, an angry mob of more than 2,000 students attempted to block his entry. Two people were killed, and many others wounded in the ensuing chaos. This forced United States Attorney General Robert F. Kennedy to send 31,000 federal troops to Mississippi.

Despite the fierce resistance, Meredith became the first black student to attend Ole Miss on October 1, 1962. Since the university accepted the course credits he had earned from Jackson State College, Meredith graduated the following year with a degree in political science. In later years, he became a political activist and authored several children's books.

The incident at Ole Miss was not the only violent battle in the Deep South over integration of higher education. By 1963, Alabama was the only state that had not desegregated its education system. Governor

George Wallace had made fighting desegregation the central theme of his gubernatorial campaign. In his 1963 inaugural address, the newly elected governor promised his white followers, "Segregation now! Segregation tomorrow! Segregation forever!" Moreover, he vowed to personally stand in the doorway to any schoolhouse in Alabama that was ordered to desegregate.

In June 1963, Wallace got the chance to keep his vow. When two black students attempted to desegregate the University of Alabama in Tuscaloosa, Wallace stood flanked by state troopers, and, in defiance of a federal mandate, literally blocked the door of the enrollment office and refused to allow the two students to register. The governor's action prompted President John F. Kennedy to deploy federal troops to the University of Alabama on June 10, 1963, to force its desegregation. The next day Governor Wallace yielded to the federal pressure and allowed Vivian Malone and James A. Hood to enroll.

Chapter Summary

At some point, virtually all of us have recited the Pledge of Allegiance to this great country. That pledge was written in 1887 and revised on four occasions over the course of a 67-year period. Despite some minor revisions to the language, the words "indivisible, with liberty and justice for all" remained in each iteration. Ironically, in 1954 – the same year the *Brown* decision was rendered – the words "under God" were added to the pledge.

The *Plessy* decision in 1896 effectively and legally divided the indivisible United States of America. In many states, primarily in the Deep South, communities pledged their allegiance to the tenets of Jim Crow, which contained blatant distortions of the tenets of the Holy Bible. They wanted separation, injustice, and inequality, especially in education. Many whites did not want black Americans to become educated because they feared blacks would challenge white supremacy. However, the notion of white supremacy was challenged, and black Americans proceeded to pursue equality and justice through education.

The pathway to those challenges ran through the federal courts with the initial focus in the field of higher education. Many all-white universities in the Deep South had the open support of state and local officials to stand in defiance of court-ordered decrees to integrate their campuses. They simply did not want African American and white students to "mingle" in any state-supported educational setting. Despite episodes of violence, which resulted in the federal government having to deploy armed troops to many college campuses in the early 1960s – many institutions of higher education in the Deep South reluctantly began to enroll black students.

While white resistance to the desegregation of public schools in the Deep South was not as violent, it was just as fierce. In its landmark *Brown* decision of 1954 and in the spirit of "one Nation under God" – the United States Supreme Court declared that state laws establishing separate public schools for black and white students were unconstitutional. In 1960, six-year-old Ruby Bridges became the first black student to integrate an all-white elementary school in the Deep South.

The legal institutional racism that existed during the Jim Crow era "shackled" black Americans and perpetuated a passive acceptance of "separate-and-unequal" education. Things began to change during the Civil Rights era when resistance to segregation was launched through America's judicial system. Because of Thurgood Marshall's tenacity; the wisdom of the nine justices on the Supreme Court in 1954; the courage of students like Ruby Bridges, the Little Rock Nine, and James Meredith; as well as the executive leadership of Presidents Dwight D. Eisenhower and John F. Kennedy – America's education system became less separate and more equal.

CHAPTER 3

Equal-but-Unwanted in Higher Education During the Affirmative Action Era

Even though the Supreme Court had ruled in the 1954 *Brown v Board of Education* case that segregation in schools was inherently unequal, there had only been incremental efforts to desegregate public schools and universities in the subsequent decade. Consequently, the Civil Rights Act of 1964 was signed into law by President Johnson. This law required schools to take actual steps to end segregation, whether it occurred by busing, redistricting, or creating magnet schools. Although the doors to many previously segregated institutions were opened to blacks because of this law, most white-controlled institutions did not welcome them—African Americans were simply "unwanted."

In a 1965 speech, President Johnson acknowledged the challenges that many black students would face when they entered all-white schools for the first time. He said, "You do not take a person who, for years, has been hobbled by chains and liberate him, bring him up to the starting line of a race and then say you are free to compete with all the others, and just believe that you are completely fair."

Those challenges were similar to the ones freed slaves encountered during the Reconstruction Era (1865 to 1877). Although the former slaves were legally free, they remained in economic, social, and educational bondage due to institutional racism and discrimination. Thus, in 1865, President Lincoln signed a bill that created a federal agency known as the Freedman's Bureau to oversee the difficult transition of African Americans from slavery to freedom.

Similarly, in the 1960s and 1970s, blacks needed some form of assistance to help break down barriers and level the playing field when the wholesale integration of America's educational system took effect. One approach to address this issue was through *affirmative action*—a term introduced by President Kennedy in a 1961 executive order to eliminate discrimination in employment practices. In 1965, President Johnson expanded affirmative action to ensure that disadvantaged groups – such as "equal-but-unwanted" African American students – had opportunities to gain access to institutions of higher education.

The primary purpose of affirmative action was to encourage predominantly white institutions to relax their admissions criteria to facilitate the enrollment of more black students. While the goal of this legislative action was to open doors for blacks, other actions like Proposition 48, which will be discussed later in this chapter, appeared to close them. Instead of focusing on admissions criteria such as grade-point averages and scores on the Scholastic Aptitude Test (SAT), programs in the Higher Education Act were created to provide financial assistance to students from low income families. All these legislative initiatives were designed to help disadvantaged students in their pursuit of the elusive American Dream.

In his 1931 book titled *Epic of America*, James Truslow Adams described the proverbial American Dream as an opportunity "in which life should be better and richer and fuller for everyone" according to their achievement or ability, not their race, creed, or color. A clear pathway to that elusive dream is a college degree. For many disadvantaged Americans, barriers related to poverty and discrimination have impeded pathways to obtaining a college degree. This chapter will examine four "actions" that have been used to remove or mitigate barriers for black Americans in their pursuit of a college degree. Those actions are: 1) Affirmative Action legislation, 2) Proposition 48 legislation, 3) financial aid, and 4) hard work. Let's examine these areas.

The Impact of Affirmative Action

In 1965, only 5 percent of the undergraduate students, 1 percent of law students, and 2 percent of medical students in the United States were African American. Things began to change after President Johnson signed his executive order related to affirmative action. In subsequent years, colleges and universities began to restructure their admissions policies to use Affirmative Action policies to increase their enrollment of minority students and staff. In many cases, the racial integration of higher education was not only swift, but it was also dramatic. For example, the number of black students in the freshmen class at Harvard University increased from a mere 9 in 1962 to an impressive 121 in 1969.

During the period of Affirmative Action, a similar pattern of increased black enrollment existed at other prestigious institutions. In 1968, there were only 31 black freshmen at Yale, and there were 96 the following year in 1969. Throughout the 1970s, black student enrollment increased at all the nation's most selective institutions, including some in the South like Duke, Rice, Emory, and the University of Virginia. While Affirmative Action played a significant role in opening doors for minority students to attend predominantly white colleges and universities, the novelty wore off and the concept gradually began to take a new meaning. Critics began to equate it with unwanted "quotas" and "reverse discrimination."

In 1978, issues related to Affirmative Action received national attention via a California court case. After two unsuccessful attempts to gain admission into the medical school at the University of California at Davis, Allan Bakke, a white man, filed suit against the university. At that time as part of its Affirmative Action Program, the university had reserved 16 of its enrollment slots for minority applicants. Bakke, citing evidence that his grades and test scores surpassed those of many minority students who had been accepted for admission, charged the medical school with "reverse discrimination" based on his race.

On June 28, 1978, the Supreme Court in *Regents of the University of California* declared Affirmative Action *constitutional* but invalidated the use of racial quotas. In other words, the Court, in a highly fragmented ruling (six separate opinions were issued), agreed that the university's use of strict racial quotas was unconstitutional and ordered the medical school to admit Bakke. However, in what could be viewed as a possible disclaimer, the Court also stipulated that institutions of higher education could use race as one criterion in their decisions to admit students.

The Bakke decision was received with mixed reactions. Many Affirmative Action supporters called the Court's ruling a stunning setback because it ruled in favor of Bakke. Many Affirmative Action opponents were concerned that the ruling had legitimized the use of race as a criterion in decisions on school admissions. Affirmative Action critics believed that by making race more relevant in admissions decisions, the weight of individual merit was diminished, which could lead to a decline in academic standards.

The varying viewpoints surrounding the Bakke case reflected the "equal-but-unwanted" mind-set that many officials in predominantly white colleges and universities espoused during that time. Overtly, many educators would claim that Affirmative Action gave black students "equal" access to opportunities that were previously afforded to white students only. Covertly, many white officials and policymakers derided Affirmative Action as an undeserved entitlement that was given to African American students who were "unwanted" and unwelcome on their campuses.

The conflicting mind-sets related to Affirmative Action can be explained using the theory of cognitive dissonance. According to this theory, a state of mental conflict is triggered when there is an inconsistency between people's beliefs or opinions (i.e., cognitions) and their attitudes or behaviors (i.e., dissonance). The inconsistency in higher education regarding Affirmative Action was manifested in the cognition or belief that black students should be given equality in education. This belief, however, was accompanied by dissonance or behavior that discriminated against black students. Theoretically, whenever this inconsistency occurs, something must change to eliminate the dissonance or behavior/attitude. Unfortunately, many officials in higher education (past and present) have refused to change their views on Affirmative Action.

Despite the controversy, the Bakke decision did not have a significant impact on the number of minority students who enrolled in schools of medicine and law. In fact, from 1978 to 1988, enrollment figures increased slightly. (See Table 1.) In 1978, an estimated 3,587 blacks were enrolled in American medical schools, which represented 6 percent of their enrollment. In 1988, the figure was 3,968, also 6 percent. A similar trend existed for blacks enrolled in the nation's law schools. In 1978, an estimated 5,304 blacks were enrolled in law schools across America, which represented 4.7 percent of the enrollment. In 1988, the figure rose to 6,028, or 5.1 percent.

Table 1

Black Student Enrollment

Medical and Law School

1978–1988

School	1978	1988	+/-
Medical	3,587	3,968	+381
Law	5,304	6,028	+724

Source: The New York Times, *July 13, 1988.*

Moving into the twenty-first century, the ongoing heated debate related to Affirmative Action has continued. Not surprisingly, the core of the debate centers around the race factor. Proponents of Affirmative Action argue that it:

- Is a way to ensure that diversity is obtained and maintained in schools
- Gives everyone an equal playing field
- Is a way to compensate for the many years of racial oppression.

Opponents of Affirmative Action argue that it:

- Is reverse discrimination
- Destroys the idea of meritocracy and makes race the main factor
- Puts students into a position who are not ready for the task

The Supreme Court's *Bakke* decision encouraged Affirmative Action goals by enabling colleges and universities to use race and other factors in academic achievement as acceptable admissions criteria. In subsequent decisions across the next several decades, courts limited the scope of Affirmative Action programs, and currently eight states (viz., Arizona, California, Florida, Michigan, Nebraska, New Hampshire, Oklahoma, and Washington) prohibit Affirmative Action programs that use race as an admissions or acceptance criterion. However, many institutions across America continue to aggressively admit members of minority groups as a matter of their predilections rather than a matter of law.

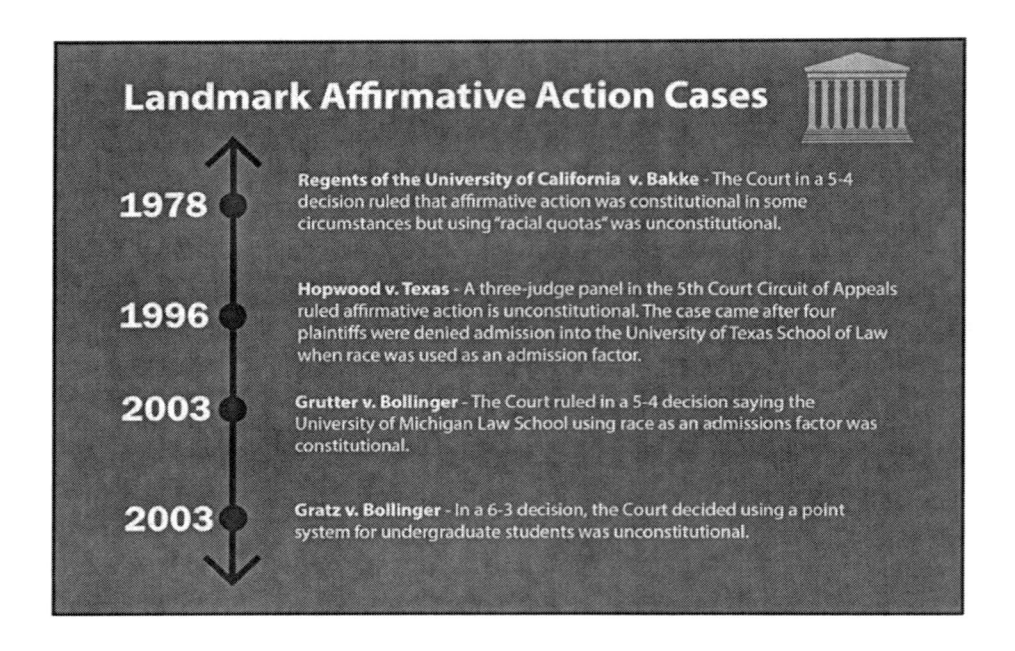

Landmark Affirmative Action Cases

1978 — **Regents of the University of California v. Bakke** - The Court in a 5-4 decision ruled that affirmative action was constitutional in some circumstances but using "racial quotas" was unconstitutional.

1996 — **Hopwood v. Texas** - A three-judge panel in the 5th Court Circuit of Appeals ruled affirmative action is unconstitutional. The case came after four plaintiffs were denied admission into the University of Texas School of Law when race was used as an admission factor.

2003 — **Grutter v. Bollinger** - The Court ruled in a 5-4 decision saying the University of Michigan Law School using race as an admissions factor was constitutional.

2003 — **Gratz v. Bollinger** - In a 6-3 decision, the Court decided using a point system for undergraduate students was unconstitutional.

One of the harshest Affirmative Action critics has come from a black man who has served on the United States Supreme Court since October 1991—Justice Clarence Thomas. In a 1995 ruling, he argued for an immediate end to Affirmative Action programs. Ironically, this black man who grew up in rural poverty-stricken Pin Point, Georgia—benefited from the program he has attempted to dismantle. As an undergraduate student at the College of the Holy Cross, Thomas received a scholarship that was set aside for racial minorities. In 1971, he was admitted to Yale Law School as part of an Affirmative Action Program that also offered him substantial financial aid. Undoubtedly, despite his current views, Affirmative Action has served Clarence Thomas well.

At some point in 2017, Justice Thomas and the U.S. Supreme Court are expected to rule in another milestone case regarding the constitutionality of Affirmative Action. The original lawsuit in that impending case was filed on behalf of Abigail Fisher, a woman who claims that she was denied admission to the University of Texas because she is white. However, according to a story in the *Huffington Post* (June 23, 2017), research indicates that Affirmative Action helps white women as much as or even more than it helps men and women of color. Ostensibly, Fisher is precisely the kind of person Affirmative Action helps the most in America today.

My Personal Experience with Affirmative Action

During my senior year at all-black C. A. Johnson High School (CAJ) in Columbia, South Carolina, my college future was set—I would be attending Howard University on an academic scholarship. The thought of matriculating in Washington, D.C. was exciting, and I saved money to help defray some of the costs not covered by the scholarship. However, things changed due to an Affirmative Action-like initiative that was unveiled in South Carolina at that time, and I never attended Howard.

In 1966, the University of South Carolina (USC) launched a full-scale effort to recruit and attract more black students by relaxing some of its admissions criteria. Although there were a few black students already enrolled, the university wanted to improve its image and diversity by giving more opportunities for minority students to attend. Thus, black students were given the opportunity to enroll in the university with an SAT score of 750 or higher instead of the minimum 900.

Now, let's shift back to my senior year at CAJ. Approximately two months before graduation, my guidance counselor summoned me to her office to discuss a proposed change in my plans to attend Howard University. After a series of discussions that involved me, my mother, and my mentor (Mr. Earl Reuben), I was persuaded to attend USC because my "success" in that environment would encourage other black students to enroll in subsequent years. In 1966, I was 1 of 10 handpicked students (7 males and 3 females) from CAJ who were included in the first wave of black students from throughout the state to attend USC.

During my freshman year at the university (which had an enrollment of approximately 25,000 students), I had little doubt that the social and academic progress of the small number of black students (i.e., less than 100) on campus was being monitored. As part of each class, all students were required to complete a 5" × 8" index card that asked for information such as the name of the high school you attended and the score you earned on the SAT. My score of 875 paled in comparison to the scores of 1,000+ that were reported by my white colleagues. Arguably, an SAT can predict academic potential; however, it did not measure three factors that resonated in me and my nine classmates from C.A.J.—pride, tenacity, and determination!

Despite occasional episodes of discrimination (especially with grading) and feelings of being unwanted, seven of the original "CAJ Ten" graduated from USC in 1970. Three of the 10 had transferred to HBCUs during their sophomore year. Each of the remaining graduates eventually earned an advanced degree and achieved success in their chosen field. Our enrollment in the university via "relaxed" admissions criteria did not provide a "crutch" or any other safeguards to ensure our success. If anything, we had to work harder to overcome episodes of subtle discrimination, especially when it involved a professor's subjectivity in grading.

Regardless of what it was called—affirmative action or recruitment—an opportunity was given for me to matriculate at USC, and I took full advantage of it. In most instances, despite having an SAT score of 875, I outperformed many of my white colleagues who had higher scores. Moreover, in 1978, I became the first African American to earn a doctoral degree in school psychology from the University of South Carolina.

Proposition 48

Proposition 48 was another form of legislation with quasi-Affirmative Action principles that ultimately had a positive impact on black students in higher education. The National Collegiate Athletic Association (NCAA) enacted this rule in 1986, and it remains in effect today. According to the rules, incoming freshmen athletes must score at least 700 out of a possible 1,600 points on the SAT or 15 out of 36 on the American College Test. In addition, the athletes must have a cumulative 2.0 grade-point average in 11 core curriculum classes. Student-athletes who do not meet these standards can still accept a grant and enroll in school. However, if they accept a grant-in-aid, they will lose a year of their athletic eligibility.

Initially, many black-student athletes lost a year of eligibility due to an inability to meet the standards of Proposition 48. In 1987, the average SAT score nationally for all students was 906. The average score for blacks was 728. The football programs at many universities, especially HBCUs, suffered due to the academic requirements imposed by Proposition 48. In 1987, Alcorn State and Bethune Cookman each had 12 recruits (the most in the nation) that were ineligible to play during their freshman year. Alabama State and Grambling were tied for third with 8 each. Three predominately white universities (Mississippi, Southern Mississippi, and Southwestern Louisiana) were tied for second with 7 each.

During the first decade of implementation, many coaches and educators decried the SAT as being culturally biased. Perhaps it was, but I believe it was a blessing in disguise. It forced many young black athletes, especially males, in high school to study harder if they wanted to play sports at the collegiate level. In doing so, they began to discard the stereotypes associated with being a dumb jock and embraced the respect associated with being a "scholar-athlete."

By the 1990s, the transformation had occurred; many young African American athletes had adopted a mind-set of becoming scholars. Cory Booker, a star athlete at Northern Valley Regional High School at Old Tappan in New Jersey, exemplified that new mind-set. He accepted a scholarship to play football at Stanford University; graduated in 1991 with a Bachelor of Arts degree in political science; earned a Master of Arts degree from Stanford in 1992; was awarded the prestigious Rhodes Scholarship in 1992 to attend Oxford University in England; and he graduated from Oxford in 1994 with a high honors degree in history. But that's not all. He also earned a Juris Doctor from the Yale Law School in 1997; and in 2013 Booker became the first black United States Senator for New Jersey.

Senator Booker is only one of many examples of countless African American student-athletes who elevated their academic game in high school during the Proposition 48 era and became scholar-athletes in college. Four other notable world-class scholar-athletes during that era included David Robinson (10-time NBA All-Star and graduate of the United States Naval Academy); Nnenna Lynch (NCAA 3,000-meter champion who became a Rhodes Scholar in 1992); Eddie George (1995 Heisman Trophy winner who earned an executive MBA at Northwestern University); and Dominique Dawes (1996 Olympics gold medal winner in gymnastics and honor graduate of the University of Maryland).

On a different note, the story of Dexter Manley is a sobering reminder of how athletes were easily exploited prior to the relatively high academic expectations that were imposed by Proposition 48. Manley was a star high school football player in Houston, Texas. Upon his graduation in 1977, he received scholarship offers from 37 colleges to play football. He accepted the offer from Oklahoma State University (OSU) and played varsity football there for four years. All of this happened despite one not-so-little caveat—Manley could not read!

Sadly, years later, officials at OSU acknowledged they were aware that Dexter was illiterate. The school's academic advisor, Dale Roark, admitted he knew Manley could not read a textbook and that OSU exploited him for four years. Roark justified the school's actions as sort of a *quid pro quo*. In other words, from their perspective, OSU gave Manley the opportunity to play four years of college football, which enabled him to be drafted by the Washington Redskins of the National Football League (NFL) in 1981.

EDUCATING DEXTER

All-Pro Defensive End Dexter Manley Talks about Football, Fatherhood, Cocaine Addiction and Learning to Read at Age 28

Dexter Manley and Tom Friend

Despite having a second-grade reading level, Manley had a stellar 11-year career in professional football. He was on two Super Bowl championship teams, and he was named to the NFL's All-Pro team in 1986. However, in his book *Educating Dexter*, he recalls the embarrassment he felt when teammates teased him about his inability to read. In one situation, he was sitting near his locker pretending to read the *Wall Street Journal* when Joe Theismann, the team's star quarterback, said, "Get the funnies Dexter, you can't read." Manley's book chronicles the bitterness and frustrations he experienced due to his inability to read, despite the success and stardom he experienced on the football field.

Who knows? Maybe the Dexter Manley story would have been different in the Proposition 48 era. Perhaps the faculty and staff in his high school would have been more focused on providing academic rigor and supports to ensure that their star athlete obtained the minimum standards that were required to play college football. Although Manley still could have played football at OSU under Proposition 48, he would not have been allowed to play during his freshman year. That would have given him a full year to at least focus on improving his less-than-marginal academic skills.

Again, who knows what would have happened? Unfortunately, what ultimately happened in the Dexter Manley saga was an all-too-familiar tragedy with uneducated black males. At the age of 36, he was convicted of cocaine possession and sentenced to four years in prison; he served two.

Financial Aid

Perhaps the most compelling form of Affirmative Action for African American students came in the form of financial aid. Poverty was one of the greatest obstacles to blacks who wanted to enroll in any institution of higher education. Poverty was widespread in black communities, and most high school graduates simply could not afford to attend college without some sort of financial assistance.

As part of his famous War on Poverty, President Lyndon Johnson triggered the creation of Affirmative Action-like policies and programs that were designed to reduce educational inequities by improving college access and affordability, especially for low-income students. In 1965, the president signed the Higher Education Act (HEA) into law. The HEA created federal assistance programs such as the Pell Grant, student loans, and Federal Work Study, which made it possible for many low-income black students to attend college.

Since the 1970s, on-campus Federal Work Study programs have provided countless low-income black students with money to help defray their college expenses. Research findings regarding the overall benefits of the program have been rather inconclusive. However, the common theme has been that working more than 20 hours per week led to decreased academic performance. Yet, working in general did not necessarily have a negative impact on grades. Not surprisingly, regardless of one's ethnicity, the greatest academic benefit to students occurred when their on-campus work study job was related to their major because it provided hands-on experience beyond the classroom.

Although small government loans have been available to black students since the late 1960s, there have been many occasions when repaying the debt was stressful and difficult. A high debt load often led black students to drop out of college, which made it more difficult to repay the loans. Black Congressman Elijah Cummings, a Democrat from Maryland, has raised national awareness of the potential adverse impact of student loans. While he acknowledges the fact that going to college can be a pathway for black students to have access to high-paying jobs, he expresses concerns that college debt can lead to financial instability.

Unlike student loans, the Pell Grant is "debt-free"—the financial award does not have to be repaid. The Pell Grant, which provides up to $5,000 per year based on financial need, has had the greatest impact on college enrollment for low-income students. Since 1972, the number of low-income students that received Pell Grants increased from 1.9 to 9.8 million students in 2013. Annually, this grant helps more than 60 percent of black undergraduates attend school and about 90 percent of all HBCU students.

Contrary to a popular belief, white students have benefited more from Pell grants than black students. According to the Pell Institute's 2013 Annual Report, 36.3 percent of the Pell Grants were awarded to white students as compared to 27.6 percent for black students. (See Table 2.) Moreover, females (62.2 percent) were awarded more grants than males (37.8 percent).

Since the late 1960s, our country has united under the ethos that every American should, if they desire, be able to go to college. For blacks, a bachelor's degree can help to mitigate any difference in economic mobility when compared to their white peers. For the average American, a bachelor's degree will add about $1 million to their lifetime earnings. Programs authorized in the HEA, such as student loans, Federal Work Study, and the Pell Grant, have made it possible for many low-income students—especially in black communities—to achieve their dream of getting a college education.

Table 2

Pell Recipients by Race in 2013

Ethnic Group	Percentage of Grants
White	36.3
Black	27.6
Hispanic	24.7
Asian	5.7
Multi-Racial	2.8
Other	1.6
Native Alaskan	0.9
Pacific Islander	0.4

Source: Pell Institute Report June 2013

Hard Work

The fourth and, arguably, strongest pathway to a college degree is through good old-fashioned hard work. In the words of Helen Keller, "If you can dream it, you can do it." People like Dr. John Edgar Wideman, Dr. Carla Peterman, and Dr. Myron Rolle dreamed of having a successful career, and they studied hard to achieve that outcome. Through hard work, each of these African American scholars earned the prestigious Rhodes Scholarship to study at Oxford University.

Wideman emerged from modest means in Pittsburgh, Pennsylvania, to attend the University of Pennsylvania where he became an All-Ivy League basketball player. After his graduation, he became the second black man in history to earn the renowned scholarship. Wideman graduated from Oxford in 1966 and continued his studies at the University of Iowa. Dr. Wideman has written 20 books, and he is a professor emeritus at Brown University. All through hard work!

Carla Peterman, a native of Oakland, California, was accepted into Yale University, but she chose to matriculate at Howard University to gain the "black experience." Through hard work and a passion to succeed, she became the first African American female graduate of an HBCU to earn the honor of being a Rhodes Scholar in 1998. At Oxford, she earned her MBA and later earned a PhD in energy and resources from the University of California at Berkeley. Peterman was also the first African American to be appointed to the California Public Utilities Commission. Dr. Peterman's accomplishments did not occur because of her race or gender—they were due to hard work!

In many aspects, the story of NFL player Myron Rolle offers some emotional relief to the Dexter Manley tragedy. Rolle's family migrated to America from the Bahamas in the middle-1980s. He excelled in academics and athletics in high school; played college football at Florida State; earned a Rhodes Scholarship in 2009; and he played in the NFL. After three years, he abruptly left the NFL to pursue a degree in medicine. In May 2017, Rolle graduated from the Florida State University College of Medicine.

Later that year, he was accepted to a neurosurgery residency at the Massachusetts General Hospital and Harvard Medical School. The primary Affirmative Action in Dr. Myron Rolle's story is pure and simple—hard work!

If academically gifted Rhodes Scholars like Drs. Wideman, Peterman, and Rolle had to work hard, then non-Rhodes Scholars had to work even harder. Shaquille "Shaq" O'Neal is one of two people whose story I will briefly cite to hopefully inspire readers. In 1992, Shaq left Louisiana State University (LSU) after three years to begin his career as a professional basketball player in the National Basketball Association (NBA). He was named Rookie of the Year in 1992, Most Valuable Player in 1999, and selected to be part of the All-NBA Team a total of 14 times. These are impressive accolades that any professional athlete would treasure.

Yet, despite achieving international acclaim as an athlete and television personality, Shaq is most proud of what he accomplished away from the basketball court and the entertainment world. In 2000, he fulfilled a promise to his mother by returning to LSU to earn his bachelor's degree. In 2005, he continued his education by earning an MBA through an online program. In 2012, Shaq received a doctoral degree in human resource development.

Finally, in my opinion, the person who exemplifies the concept of working harder to achieve success during the era when blacks were equal-but-unwanted is actress Viola Davis. She was born in 1965 on her grandmother's farm on the then-Singleton Plantation in racially segregated St. Matthews, South Carolina. Shortly after her birth, Viola's father moved the family to Central Falls, Rhode Island, to flee the oppression of racism in the Deep South. Her mother had an eighth-grade education and worked as a maid, and her father only had a fifth-grade education and worked as a horse groomer.

Viola and her family were the only African Americans in their community. She grew up in poverty and had to contend with a great deal of racial prejudice as a child. Her classmates teased her unmercifully because of her race and appearance. During an emotional interview with

US Magazine in March 2015, Viola recounted the struggles she experienced as a child in a low-income family. She said, "I didn't know where the next meal was coming from. I did everything to get food."

After graduating from Central Falls High School, Viola studied at Rhode Island College where she earned a bachelor's degree in theatre in 1988. She then attended the prestigious Julliard School of Drama in New York for four years where she received awards and recognition for her exceptional talent in the performing arts. In 2002, Rhode Island College awarded Viola an honorary doctorate in Fine Arts. Clearly, this African American woman ascended the ladder of success by working harder than her peers.

Let's hit the reset button and take another look at Viola and the personal challenges she encountered along her pathway to educational success. First, although she came from a low-income family, she did not allow her impoverished circumstances to destroy her dream of earning a college degree. Therefore, she sought and obtained financial assistance that enabled her to attend Rhode Island College. Second, and most importantly, Viola worked harder than her peers. It enabled her to overcome barriers (racial discrimination, feelings of being unwanted, etc.) that otherwise would have dashed her hopes of ever achieving a college education.

I conclude by stating the obvious—Viola Davis has achieved far more than three college degrees. She is an icon who has achieved the ultimate American Dream. As an actress, she ranks among the greatest of all time. Since making her screen debut with a small role in the 1996 film *Substance of Fire*, Viola has become the only black actress to win the triple crown of acting, which includes an Academy, Emmy, and Tony Awards. In the words of Retired General Colin Powell, "A dream does not become a reality through magic; it takes, sweat, determination and hard work."

Chapter Summary

During the Affirmative Action Era (1965–1999), there were four positive resources available to help African Americans mitigate the barriers of discrimination that blocked or impeded their pathway to a college degree.

One opportunity was provided through Affirmative Action programs. Essentially, these were a series of policies or programs that were designed to give special consideration for college admission to members of historically excluded groups such as minorities and women. Although affirmative action paved the way for many blacks to attend predominantly white colleges and universities, it also became a hotly debated issue. Opponents of the policy often referred to it as *reverse discrimination*. Yet, Affirmative Action supporters viewed it as a strategy to redress the history of college admissions policies that had discriminated against blacks and other minority groups.

Black enrollment in predominantly white colleges and universities soared in the 1970s. Many institutions of higher education embraced the Affirmative Action principles and used them to improve student diversity on their campuses. Despite the Supreme Court's 1978 *Bakke* decision, which ruled that Affirmative Action was constitutional but racial quotas were not, colleges and universities continued their efforts to recruit black students by relaxing their admissions criteria. These actions enabled many blacks to pursue the American Dream of earning a college degree to improve their economic and social status.

While many African American students took advantage of Affirmative Action to gain admission into prestigious institutions, they still had to perform in the classroom, and, in most instances, they performed quite well. One prominent black official, Justice Clarence Thomas, has openly distanced himself from anything related to Affirmative Action. His greatest fear was to have anyone question the legitimacy of his academic accomplishments as something given to him courtesy of Affirmative Action. Although Affirmative Action cannot and did not guarantee success, it did open many doors. Undoubtedly, success or failure was (and is) contingent on the individual person who walks through those open doors.

Athletic scholarships provided a second pathway to college for blacks. The impact of *Proposition 48* cannot be understated in terms of the impact it had on transforming the mind-set of black high school athletes. Under this proposition, which was enacted in 1986, the NCAA required all incoming freshmen athletes to have a minimum grade point average of 2.0 and a score of at least 700 on the SAT to be eligible to receive an athletic scholarship. Student-athletes who failed to meet those academic standards were ineligible to participate in NCAA-sanctioned competition during their freshman year, and they had to pay their own tuition during that year.

The initial reaction to Proposition 48 in the black community was largely negative. The new academic standards were chided as being discriminatory and enacted to deny black students the opportunity to receive athletic scholarships for college. If the intent of the new standards was to suppress black participation in college sports, it was not successful. On the contrary, these new standards compelled black student-athletes in high schools to study harder, and they did. By 1996, a transformation had occurred, and black student-athletes had begun to meet the NCAA requirements with little difficulty. Simply put, they rose to the level of expectation.

Financial aid in the form of student loans and Pell Grants provided the third pillar-of-help for disadvantaged students to pursue the American Dream. Many low-income black students took advantage of federal dollars that became available to assist with the cost of college tuition. Annually, over 60 percent of all black students who attend college receive financial assistance though federally funded work study programs, Pell Grants, and/or student loans. Since most student loans result in the accumulation of debt that must be repaid, they are more of a hand-up than a hand-out.

The final and most powerful action available to African American students to mitigate barriers on their path to achieving an education remains the same. There is no substitute for *hard work*. Unlike government-controlled Affirmative Action and financial aid programs, the individual student controls the amount of work or effort he or she is willing to invest toward achieving success. Despite barriers that involved discrimination and poverty, people like Viola Davis, Oprah Winfrey, and Tyler Perry achieved their American Dream through determination, perseverance, and hard work.

CHAPTER 4

Report Card for America's Education System During the Twentieth Century

Oppression occurs in societies when targeted groups of people are pushed down or discriminated against. The word comes from the Latin root *opprimere*, which means "pressed down." Some ways in which people in a society tend to be pushed down or discriminated against include but are not limited to:

- Sexism (when women are pushed down)
- Classism (when the poor are pushed down)
- Ableism (when the disabled are pushed down)
- Nativism (when immigrants are pushed down)
- Racism (when people from a specific race are pushed down)

In many cases, these categories overlap in such a way that one person may have to deal with multiple forms of oppression. For example, a low-income black female would have to deal with three forms of oppression—classism, racism, and sexism. In many cases, members of the oppressed group would have difficulty performing to the best of their ability, especially if they had been treated as inferior on an ongoing basis. This was the plight of blacks during the oppressive period of racial segregation in America during most of the twentieth century.

In 1868, the 14th Amendment to the U.S. Constitution gave blacks full citizenship and promised them equal protection under the law. Blacks voted, won elected offices, and even served on juries. However, 10 years later, federal troops were withdrawn from the South and the local government returned to white rule. By 1890, blacks lost almost all they had gained under the 14th Amendment, and Jim Crow laws, which were based on the theory of white supremacy, became legal. This marked the beginning of the racist period of harsh legal discrimination against black Americans.

Under the leadership of Thurgood Marshal and the NAACP, this segregationist concept of "separate-but-equal" public schools was defeated in the Supreme Court in 1954. In subsequent years, the Civil Rights Act of 1964 opened the doors of predominantly white institutions to blacks; federal programs like Affirmative Action forced those institutions to adjust their admissions criteria to accommodate black applicants; and federally funded programs like the Pell Grant provided financial assistance for low-income students to attend college.

While federal intervention was needed to redress many evils of the great oppression, black institutions were in an uphill battle and continuously lagged behind white institutions in four key components of public and higher education. Those four key components include school facilities, resources, achievement, and teacher training. This chapter provides a critical analysis of the progress (or lack thereof) that was made with each component during the period of oppression in the twentieth century.

School Facilities

Given the oppressive economic and social challenges that black communities faced entering the twentieth century, one can only imagine the condition of their schools. In a 1917 report compiled by the American Council on Education, we are given a glimpse of what those schools were like. Many of the school buildings for blacks had leaking roofs, sagging floors, and windows without glass. The dilapidated facilities ranged from being untidy to outright filthy and unsafe. In addition, the classrooms were crowded, and typically all grades were taught in the same room by one teacher.

Unexpectedly, one of the greatest positive impacts on the reformation of school facilities for black children during that oppressive Jim Crow era was due to the efforts of a white man named Julius Rosenwald. This multimillionaire president of Sears, Roebuck & Company took a special interest in the plight of black children and the deplorable condition of the schools they attended. Thus, he created a charity named the Rosenwald Foundation that committed large sums of money in 15 Southern states for the construction of safe comfortable schools affectionately called the Rosenwald Schools. Over the course of nearly two decades (1917–1932), this foundation contributed to the construction of over 5,000 school buildings, nearly 200 teachers' homes, and five industrial high schools for black students. Ultimately, hundreds of thousands of black children received a good education in the Rosenwald Schools.

Mr. Rosenwald also supported higher education for black students. He became a trustee of Tuskegee Institute and befriended Booker T. Washington. A humanitarian, Rosenwald donated over two million dollars for facility improvements at Tuskegee, Howard, Fisk, and Dillard Universities. Through his philanthropy, he also played a huge role in providing opportunities for many black students to learn in a safe, healthy, and stimulating school environment.

As evidenced by the philanthropy of Rosenwald, improvements to school facilities require money, and throughout the first half of the "separate but unequal" twentieth century, blacks simply did not have access to the funding needed to build first-class schools. After the Supreme Court issued its *Brown v Board of Education* decision in 1954, the expectation was that school facilities for blacks and whites would be equally funded by state and local authorities. Although that expectation was met with stiff resistance, local and state authorities unwittingly provided additional funding to black districts for school improvements.

In response to the *Brown* decision, many southern states adopted equalized school funding programs for black and white schools as a strategy to avoid integration. In South Carolina, for example, the state launched a $75-million campaign in 1960 to build schools under the guise of improving education for all children. However, the intent of equalization programs throughout the South was to try to maintain segregation by improving schools in black communities.

The construction projects for these improved school facilities were well-received in many black communities, especially in rural areas. Hundreds of schools were built throughout the South under state-funded equalization programs. Families and teachers were thrilled with their new buildings. For some, it was the first time their schools had indoor plumbing and centralized heating. Although the equalization programs did, indeed, improve school facilities in many black communities, significant problems in other areas emerged.

While equalization schools were attractive and appealing, many of them lacked gyms, football fields, and updated textbooks. Moreover, many of these equalization plans did not provide for the equalization of salaries for black and white teachers. This disparity led to several lawsuits involving equal pay and other programmatic disparities in the segregated school systems' equalization plans. Ultimately, those state-funded plans could not hold back the tide of integration. By 1975, two decades after the *Brown* decision, all states in the South had abandoned their separate-but-equalization plans and complied with federal mandates to desegregate all public schools.

Historically, the federal government played a rather small role in school funding. After the failed attempts by many southern states to maintain school segregation through their equalization plans, the federal government became more involved with school funding. In 1960, state and local governments funded 96 percent of public schools, while the federal government funded 4 percent. In 1980, state and local governments funded 90 percent of public education, while the federal government funded 10 percent. With this funding increase, the federal government assumed greater oversight of spending in public education.

In theory, by 1999, all public schools in America were integrated and equal. However, in reality they were not. According to a report by the Harvard Civil Rights Project, our nation's schools became increasingly more segregated in the 1990s. This *re-segregation* was explained in terms of "white flight" to the suburbs. As schools in the suburbs became "whiter", schools in the inner city became "browner." This *de facto* segregation has resulted in a disparity in educational finance, because school systems in the suburbs can generate more revenue through local property taxes from their more affluent residents. With more money available, school systems in the suburbs constructed better facilities. Thus, by 1999, many school facilities in rural and inner-city districts were unequal or inferior to those in affluent suburban America.

Curriculum

Educators have different perspectives regarding the definition, purpose, and types of curriculums. They do, however, tend to agree that a curriculum refers to the strategies and materials students use to interact with teachers to achieve desired educational outcomes. During the first six decades of the twentieth century, many segregated school systems with white student populations utilized two types of curriculums. First, there was the *written* curriculum, which was comprised of the documents that were produced by the state and local boards specifying what was to be taught. Then, there was the *taught* curriculum, which was the one that teachers used in the classroom.

The curriculums for segregated school systems with black student populations during that same period were different. Their two curriculums can best be described as what I call *situational* and *adaptive*. The *situational* curriculum was a quasi-written set of manual labor skills that were compiled to help the students adjust to the demands of their socio-economic environment. For example, the curriculum for poor black children that lived in a farming community focused on rudimentary skills, such as tallying, using proper techniques to grow produce, fixing farm tools, and recognizing the symptoms of diseased crops. The *adaptive* curriculum was largely unstructured, and teachers typically used their personal experiences and imagination to deliver instruction.

America's racially segregated school systems reinforced the presumption that was held by many whites through the 1940s: Blacks were inherently incapable of learning at an advanced level. Segregating white children from black children was rationalized as a means of ensuring that the educational advancement of white children would not be stymied by the presence of less-intelligent black students. Consequently, black schools were woefully underfunded, and in many instances, states did not provide them access to meaningful curriculum and instructional materials. Metaphorically speaking, while black children struggled along the path to an education in their bare feet with blinders, white children traveled the same path with the aid of a Model-T Ford and an adult navigator.

A great example of a *situational* curriculum occurred during the 1960s. In 1964, a campaign named Freedom Summer was launched in Mississippi to combat voter suppression by registering as many black voters as possible. This campaign received national support from congressmen, leaders of the Civil Rights Movement, and organizations like the Student Nonviolent Coordinating Committee (SNCC).

During that summer, members of SNCC were appalled by what they described as the *sharecropper education* that blacks received in substandard schools. In response, they created Freedom Schools throughout Mississippi to provide six weeks of relevant rigorous instruction. The curriculum they developed was designed to address the oppressed situation that blacks were facing at that time. A key element of instruction was to teach students how to become social change agents and participate in the ongoing Civil Rights

Movement. The education at these Freedom Schools was student-centered, leadership development was encouraged, and proficiency in traditional academic skills was expected.

Unlike what transpired in many black schools during the first half of the twentieth century, there was no unstructured delivery of instruction (*adaptive* curriculum) in the Freedom Schools. Many highly qualified teachers were recruited to Mississippi to teach in these schools, and they used proven instructional strategies (e.g., open discussions and lesson plans) to engage students. The United Federation of Teachers in New York sent the largest contingent of teachers to teach in the schools. During that summer, nearly 40 Freedom Schools were established and served approximately 2,500 students, including parents.

At the end of the summer of 1964, many of the students remained in the Freedom Schools rather than return to their segregated schools. The students that did return to their segregated schools learned their curriculum well; they wanted reform. These students demanded improvements, and they insisted that white educators (i.e., the superintendent and local members of the school board) include African American history and literature in their curriculum. They resisted the goals of the infamous *sharecropper* curriculum and insisted on having a curriculum that would prepare them for college.

The political awareness these Freedom students gained during that summer had a profound and lasting impact on their perspective of human and civil rights. In September 1964, after a group of students in an all-black high school in Mississippi was suspended for wearing "One Man, One Vote" buttons, the entire student body walked out and shut down the school. A court case ensued that was used as a precedent in the landmark *Tinker v Des Moines* (1969), which protected the students' right to free speech.

The legacy of the Freedom Schools was reborn under the leadership of Marian Wright Edelman, founder of the Children's Defense Fund (CDF). In 1995, sites for the first two CDF Freedom Schools were established in South Carolina and Missouri. The CDF's Freedom Schools employed a transformative curriculum that continues to serve as a model for public education systems across America. Students are expected to use high-level reasoning skills to solve problems that are relevant to their local community and the nation within a world context. Teachers are trained to have high expectations for all students and to use culturally responsive pedagogy to engage students. These high-quality strategies were not used in the oppressive, now-defunct *sharecropper* curriculum.

Achievement

Given the history of oppression in education, it should come as no surprise that there is an ongoing race gap in achievement in America. During the first half of the twentieth century, there was very little systematic testing to determine the achievement level of black students. Instead, controversial assumptions were postulated. Those assumptions were girded in a eugenics movement or mode of thinking. Essentially, the proponents of this racist mode of thinking believed that whites were biologically superior to people of color, especially those with an African heritage. These white supremacist views were prominent in Jim Crow America and Nazi Germany.

After the *Brown v Board of Education* decision in 1954, educators became more interested in standardized testing to measure the achievement levels of students in public educations. The testing movement became even more important in 1957 after the Soviet Union (USSR) launched Sputnik, the world's first artificial satellite. This launching caught the U.S. government off guard, shook the country's confidence, and marked the beginning of the space race. Americans began to question whether the country's educational system was adequate, especially in training scientists and engineers.

The space race caused a revolution in American education. The federal government encouraged school systems to include more math and science courses in their curriculums; elementary schools began to provide second language instruction; and baby-boomer families started buying educational toys such as chemistry sets and plastic models of the human body. Moreover, school systems started to place more emphasis on standardized testing programs to identify gifted students to help America reclaim its superiority over the USSR in technology.

By 1962, the space race was in full gear and the National Aeronautics and Space Administration (NASA) was actively conducting research in the field of space technology. Undoubtedly, many leaders in the nation's executive branch of government were aware of the contributions that Katherine Johnson, a black woman who worked at NASA as a human computer, was making to the space program. She helped to formulate the math that sent astronaut John Glenn into orbit and back home in 1962. Ms. Johnson's story is told in the hit movie *Hidden Figures* in which she is portrayed by actress Taraji P. Henson.

As interest in the impact of desegregation mounted and the prospect of finding more hidden jewels in public education like math-genius Katherine Johnson, a federal commission was appointed to

> This is Katherine Johnson, an American physicist and mathematician who calculated NASA's rocket flight trajectories. She was involved in the Apollo 11 mission, the Space Shuttle program, the Earth Resources Satellite, and plans for a mission to Mars.
>
> Her work was so accurate that when NASA switched to using computers, they would call on her to check the computer's calculations for errors.

examine educational equality in the United States. The commission, which was headed by sociologist James Coleman, surveyed more than 600,000 students and 60,000 teachers across 4,000 public schools. In 1966, the Coleman Report was published and included three major findings as follows:

1. School funding levels do not significantly affect student achievement, but student background and teacher effectiveness do.
2. Black students perform better in racially integrated classrooms, which led to busing-for-desegregation programs.
3. Standardized tests measure cultural knowledge, not intelligence, which puts minority students at a disadvantage.

The Coleman Report was the first to articulate the racial and economic divide between white and minority students that came to be referred to as the infamous *achievement gap*. Coleman and his coauthors concluded that academic achievement was strongly related to students' socioeconomic status, and as they progressed through school, the achievement gap widened. Moreover, the Coleman Report defended standardized tests as the most reliable measure of students' academic gains, not intelligence or aptitudes.

There were mixed reactions to the Coleman findings. Proponents of the eugenics point of view argued that this achievement gap was due to the difference in the intellectual capacities between whites and African Americans. In his 1969 article, Arthur Jensen offered statistical data to indicate that, based on IQ scores, African Americans were genetically inferior to whites. Jensen's views fueled outrage across America and rekindled mental images of Jim Crow America. I can verify that outrage existed in the black community because I was a student at the University of South Carolina when this controversial article was released.

The ongoing debates and discussions related to the space program, race, intelligence, bussing, and achievement gaps exposed the need for valid and reliable standardized testing in public education. Thus, the National Assessment Educational Progress (NAEP) was developed in 1969 to measure student achievement nationally in nine subjects in three grades (grades 4, 8, and 12). The NAEP's results are included in an annual document known as the Nation's Report Card, which is the only ongoing national assessment of how students in the United States are performing in the different subject areas.

The Nation's Report Cards have provided valuable information to foster a better understanding of the achievement gap. According to NAEP data, the reading gap between black and white 17-year-olds narrowed by more than 40 percent between 1971 and 1994. The math gap also narrowed during that period, though not quite as much. Overall, between 1970 to 1999, the achievement gap in America's schools was narrowed because black children's scores increased, not because white children's scores fell. In other words, as black children gained greater access to a quality education, their academic outcomes improved.

Teacher Effectiveness

As mentioned previously, one of the key findings in the 1969 Coleman Report was the notion that teachers matter more to student achievement than any other aspect of school. In subsequent years, this assertion became the subject of many discussions, projects, and research studies.

Invariably, educators tended to agree that when it comes to student performance on reading and math tests, a teacher is estimated to have two to three times the impact of any other school factor, including facilities, socioeconomic status, and even leadership. This positive impact on student academic performance is known as the *teacher effect*.

An effective teacher is a person who can relate to and communicate with students in a positive way to facilitate academic achievement. During the period of segregation, black teachers did not receive as much training as white teachers. Moreover, the salary for black teachers was so low that it was hard to find fully qualified ones, especially men. Undoubtedly, disparities in preparedness and training (and possibly salary) adversely impacted the effectiveness of many black teachers.

Even when states began the wholesale process of desegregating their schools, many African American teachers continued to face challenges. During the process of desegregation, numerous black schools were simply closed, and their students were bussed to white schools. In many instances, African American teachers were pushed out of the profession through demotions, firings, and forced resignations. Consequently, by 1972, more than 38,000 African American educators lost their jobs and entered another profession.

The desegregation of America's schools created an unintended (or perhaps intended) consequence—namely, a predominantly white teacher workforce. Whether intended or not, within the past three decades, 82 percent of public school teachers have come from white middle-class families. At the same time, however, the nation's students have become increasingly more diverse. This situation raised questions regarding the potential impact the diversity gap between students and teachers would have on student outcomes in public education.

What was the impact of the increase in the diversity gap between white teachers and their minority students? Does a teacher's race or cultural background really matter? Before we address these questions, let's examine perhaps the most important component of a teacher's effectiveness—student engagement. Learning is not a spectator sport. Students do not learn much by sitting idly in a classroom or memorizing esoteric assignments. Students learn when they are actively and meaningfully engaged with a caring and knowledgeable teacher. In a nutshell, *disengaged* students are those who are not learning, and *engaged* students are those who are learning.

After years of progress in the 1970s and 1980s, the achievement gap between black and white students widened in 1988. Prominent black educators such as James A. Banks and John U. Ogbu attributed this setback to the struggles many white teachers faced with attempting to engage minority students in their classrooms. They cited cultural issues, low expectations, and preexisting stereotypes as the main barriers. These scholars argued that many dimensions of pedagogy (i.e., attitudes of teachers, instructional styles, instructional materials, and policies) must undergo change to provide equal educational opportunities for students of color.

Gloria Ladson-Billings was especially interested in the instructional and cultural dimensions of public education. She believed that a hidden racism was embedded in our educational system that prevented children of color from reaching their educational potential. Thus, in 1995, she introduced the concept of culturally responsive pedagogy (CRP) as an instructional strategy to bridge the gap between white teachers and students of color. One of the central tenets of CRP is for teachers to strengthen their connections with the students' home culture while focusing on their academic achievement. This concept was well received by educators, and many school systems started to develop programs to train their teachers in the principles of CRP to improve their instructional engagement with students of color.

The answer to the to the central question of "Does a teacher's race or cultural background really matter?" is a definite yes. The cultural gap between teachers and their students can have an adverse impact on achievement. Learning occurs when teachers can actively engage their students in instruction. This process becomes more difficult when there is a cultural gap between teachers and their students.

Chapter Summary

In this chapter, four key components of public education (school facilities, curriculum, achievement, and teacher effectiveness) were examined to determine the progress black students have made in each area. The rubric found in the following table (Table 3) was created to assist with gauging the progress (or lack thereof) black students have made in each component area during the twentieth century since the passage of the Civil Rights Act in 1964. Based on this rubric, my report card for America's performance with providing a quality public education for black children is as follows:

1. Facilities = *Encouraging*
2. Curriculum = *Encouraging*
3. Achievement = *Disappointing*
4. Teacher Effectiveness = *Disappointing*

Table 3

Scoring Rubric for America's Performance with Public Education for Black Students

Component	Disappointing	Encouraging	Very Encouraging
School Facilities	**Some** black students in public education are taught in safe facilities with stimulating learning environments.	**Most** black students in public education are taught in safe facilities with stimulating learning environments.	The **vast majority** of black students in public education are taught in safe facilities with stimulating learning environments.

Component	Disappointing	Encouraging	Very Encouraging
Curriculum	**Some** black students in public education are taught using standards from rigorous and relevant curriculums.	**Most** black students in public education are taught using standards from rigorous and relevant curriculums.	The **vast majority** of black students in public education are taught using standards from rigorous and relevant curriculums.
Achievement	The achievement gap is **widening** between black and white students in public education.	The achievement gap is **narrowing** between black and white students in public education.	The achievement gap is **closing** between black and white students in public education.
Teacher Effectiveness	**Some** white teachers in public education have the skills needed to engage black students in classroom learning.	**Most** white teachers in public education have the skills needed to engage black students in classroom learning.	The **vast majority** of white teachers in public education have the skills needed to engage black students in classroom learning.

The ramifications of the report card are clear. More work is needed to address the adverse impact of the racial discrimination black students endured in public education before and during the twentieth century. While some progress has been made, vestiges of institutional racism and disparate treatment still exist. Perhaps the most pressing need is for public schools to hire and train more culturally competent teachers who can effectively engage minority students in the learning process. A bad teacher can cripple a student for years. The second part of this book will examine issues that have emerged in the 21st twenty-first century, and the last part will present strategies on how to address them.

Finally, a noteworthy bright spot in America's educational system occurred in higher education. During a 20-year period (1979–1999), the enrollment of African Americans in colleges and universities skyrocketed. This outcome was due in large part to the hard work of black families, college admissions officers, and advocates for education. This suggests that an increasing number of black American students were choosing the higher education pathway to pursue the American Dream. Therefore, I will give America's system of higher education a rating of "very encouraging" on this report card.

PART II

AMERICA'S EDUCATION SYSTEM DURING THE TWENTY-FIRST CENTURY

CHAPTER 5

Current Challenges in K–12 Public Education

The racist effort to keep African Americans uninformed and uneducated during most of the twentieth century was blatant. America was plagued by a *de jure* system of segregated schools, and in many instances, whites in the Deep South resorted to violence to maintain the status quo. As the nation moved into the twenty-first century, the days of educational and racial discrimination against black Americans appeared to have vanished. However, as typical of most illnesses, the symptoms can be disguised with some sort of medication. In America, despite the implementation of various forms of medical treatment (i.e., policies, programs, and promises), some symptoms of the twentieth century educational discrimination against African Americans still exist today, albeit in a more refined form.

In her 2010 book titled *The New Jim Crow: Mass Incarceration in the Age of Colorblindness,* Michelle Alexander argues that systemic racial discrimination in the United States has resumed in the twenty-first century. Much of this subtle or *invisible* racism is manifested in oppressive laws, policies, and practices that are designed to obstruct the pathways for African Americans that lead to the American Dream. Public education is one of those pathways.

In this chapter, we examine four major challenges in public education that either directly or indirectly impact African Americans in the twenty-first century: multiculturalism, poverty, school policies, and teaching African American males. As a country, it is imperative that educators recognize these four major challenges and not allow a system of invisible racism to destroy America's greatest resource—our children.

Multiculturalism

September 2014 marked a new era for the complexion of public schools in the United States. It was the first-time children of color constituted a majority of the students enrolled in K–12 public education nationwide. According to the National Center for Education Statistics, this trend will continue and the enrollment of white students in public schools will shrink to 46 percent. With whites now making up less than half of America's K–12 students, the country's success or failure in the twenty-first century will hinge on the ability of teachers to teach children of color in their classrooms.

Even though the complexion of student populations in America's public schools has undergone a dramatic shift in the twenty-first century, the profile of the teachers in the classrooms has remain virtually unchanged in the past 30 years. In July 2016, the U.S. Department of Education released a report titled *The State of Racial Diversity in the Educator Workforce*, which indicated that 82 percent of all teachers in public schools were white, English-speaking, and middle class. This dynamic created a culture gap between students and their teachers that can be a factor in the students' performance in school.

Dr. Wandy W. Taylor, a retired principal of a large and highly-diverse Title I elementary school in the Metropolitan Area of Atlanta, shared several harrowing stories of how the culture gap between students and teachers can create unnecessary conflict. Dr. Taylor cited an incident she observed in 2016 that involved a white female teacher providing instruction to a third-grade class with predominantly black and Hispanic students. The students were having difficulty completing what the teacher deemed a simple classroom assignment. The third graders were told to write about the things that were in their family's garage.

When the frustrated teacher lashed out at the students because of the quizzical looks on their faces, the principal asked the teacher to step outside the classroom with her for a moment. In an assuring tone, Dr. Taylor informed the teacher that the writing assignment was too abstract for many of the students because most of them lived in apartments or motels; their families did not have garages! For this assignment (and probably many others), the teacher's middle-class status and lack of cultural awareness impeded her ability to engage the students in the learning process.

Dr. Taylor further indicated that a teacher's lack of cultural competence can also impede their ability to engage parents. This principal reported an incident in which she observed how a teacher unintentionally insulted two parents during a face-to-face conference. In that scenario, the teacher told Mr. and Mrs. Zhang Tao (a pseudonym) that, "I have five other Oriental children in my class, and they are doing fine." To which Mr. Toa replied, "We are Asian; an Oriental is a rug." Needless to say, the teacher's cultural incompetence was exposed and perhaps her credibility, too.

For clarity, a distinction should be made between *cultural competence* and *multiculturalism* in education. Cultural competence refers to a skill; namely, a teacher's ability to understand and teach students from cultures other than his or her own. Multiculturalism refers to the process or training whereby teachers acquire and implement those skills. In the absence of multiculturalism, teachers are more apt to use a trial-and-error approach to connect with diverse groups of students, which is often a recipe for failure, both for the teacher and the entire school community.

The community of Bell Manor Elementary School learned this lesson the hard way, so to speak. The school, which is in the Dallas-Fort Worth area of Texas, has an enrollment of 769 students where 36 percent are white, 27 percent Hispanic, and 24 percent African American. In September 2016, the *Star-Telegram* newspaper featured an article about an incident involving a teacher's use of a racial slur at school. As reported in the article, a white female teacher divided her sixth graders into small groups to engage in a team-building exercise. Each group was assigned a nickname. One group was given the name "Dream Team" and another was dubbed the "Jighaboos". The names for the various groups were prominently displayed in the teacher's classroom on laminated paper for any and everyone to see.

After one student's father discovered this, he became livid. He contacted the local TV station and openly questioned how a teacher could be so oblivious to the fact that the word *Jighaboo* is commonly used as a racial slur for a black person. The school's administration investigated the father's complaint, confronted the teacher, and removed the posters. The school released a statement alleging the teacher was visibly shaken and remorseful, because she was not aware that Jighaboo (correct spelling is Jigaboo) was a racial slur. The teacher's defense was quite simple—ignorance.

While ignorance of a law or a policy is never a good defense, there is a cure for ignorance—knowledge. Far be it for me to question that teacher's motives because I cannot judge what is in her heart. Had she received some sort of training or professional development in multiculturalism, she would have been more culturally competent. Given the racial diversity at Bell Manor, the school's administrators should bear some culpability. As part of the school's strategic plan for pedagogy, this teacher should have received some sort of training in multicultural education to help bridge the culture gap between herself and the students. Unfortunately, this teacher's cultural incompetence created discord in her classroom engagement as well as a public relations nightmare for the entire school.

The nation's education system experienced a public relations nightmare during the 2016 presidential campaign. Donald Trump fueled a sense of xenophobia across America through his rhetoric and travel ban against Muslims. His actions influenced a wave of Trump-inspired criticism and vitriol regarding the racial diversity in our public schools. Numerous incidents were reported in which white students invoked Trump's name while engaging in racist behavior, such as telling black students to "go back to Africa", taunting Hispanic students with chants of "build that wall (along the Mexican border)", and threatening Muslim teachers.

During the height of this Trump-inspired racism in some of our nation's schools, teachers in Seattle, Washington, joined together to show their support for student diversity in their schools. On October 19, 2016, nearly 2,000 Seattle teachers reported to work wearing "Black Lives Matter" shirts and displaying banners with the words "Black Students' Lives Matter." This act of solidarity was in response to the postponement of an annual event where 100 black men were scheduled to greet all children at the school door and speak to them during an assembly. The event was allegedly postponed due to online threats made by one or more Trump-inspired white supremacists.

As evidenced by their actions, the Seattle teachers embraced diversity in their schools and received national recognition for doing so. Most importantly, teachers throughout this school system reported that their students respected the public display of support. Consequently, it enhanced the teachers' ability to engage with their students in the classroom. This public display of support for diversity exemplified some of the basic tenets of multiculturalism, such as respect for other ethnic groups, increasing awareness of global issues, and strengthening cultural consciousness. This was not a one-time show of solidarity for the Seattle teachers because, after Election Day, they donned their "Black Lives Matter" shirts once again.

By the next presidential election in 2020, the Census Bureau has indicated that more than half of the nation's children are expected to be part of a minority race or ethnic group. As our public schools continue to become more diverse, there will be increasing demand to find effective ways to help all students succeed academically as well as get along with each other. Teachers are faced with the challenge of engaging all students in meaningful instruction while not favoring one group over another.

In a 2007 study conducted by the National Comprehensive Center for Teacher Quality, nearly 70 percent of new teachers said their training in college did not prepare them to teach an ethnically diverse student body. In the absence of this preparation, the students, not the teachers, suffer the most. The ramifications of the increasing diversity in our nation's schools and the lack of teacher preparation are clear; something is needed to bridge that gap. Now, more than ever, multicultural education is a proven form of pedagogy that can be used to improve a teacher's effectiveness in racially and ethnically diverse classroom settings.

Poverty

Since the middle 1960s, one of the greatest challenges that faced K–12 public education in the United States has been how to effectively educate disadvantaged children. Title I of the 1965 Elementary and Secondary Education Act (ESEA) sought to address this problem by providing additional funding to school districts that served low-income students. Despite the additional funding, data compiled by the Center on Education Policy in 2011 indicated that students in high-diverse, high-poverty schools continued to lag behind their peers in educational outcomes such as achievement.

Before examining some specific academic outcomes, it would be prudent to offer an operational definition and some characteristics of poverty. The Children's Defense Fund describes *poverty* as a deficiency in or lack of access to necessary or desirable resources, such as money, goods, or means of support, which in turn, increase the risk of ...

- Emotional and social challenges
- Acute and chronic stressors
- Cognitive lags
- Health and safety issues

Fifty years after President Johnson declared a war on poverty, children in America continue to struggle with issues that are either directly or indirectly related to poverty. Some facts related to the ongoing impact of poverty are as follows:

- Child poverty today is only 5 percent less than in 1964.
- Gun deaths of children and teens increased 31 percent with black children five times more likely to be the victim.
- The U.S. infant mortality rate is still one of the highest among industrialized nations.
- The U.S. teen birth rate is still among the highest in industrialized nations.

- The percent of children living in single-parent households has more than doubled.
- The majority of fourth- and eighth-grade students from poor families continue to read below their grade levels.
- Black children remain three times more likely than white children to be poor.
- Children in poverty are six times more likely to drop out of high school.

The U.S. Census Bureau compiles data to determine the official poverty rate in America. Historically, the official poverty rate in the United States has ranged from a high of 22.4 percent in 1959 to a low of 11.1 percent in 1973. Based on the Census Bureau's 2017 estimates, the official poverty rate in the nation is 12.7 percent or roughly 43.1 million Americans. Among racial and ethnic groups, African Americans hold the highest poverty rate at 22.0 percent, followed by Hispanics at 19.4 percent, Asians at 10.0 percent, and whites at 8.8 percent. As stated earlier, poverty continues to have an adverse impact on children in areas such as health and academic achievement.

Typically, when the academic achievement of poverty-stricken students is measured, it is done by comparing the scores of students in Title I versus non-Title I schools. The basic principles of Title I are to provide supplemental funds to schools with large concentrations of low-income students to assist in meeting their educational goals. Low-income or disadvantaged students are determined by their eligibility to receive a free or reduced-price lunch. For an entire school to qualify for Title I funds, at least 40 percent of students must enroll in the free and reduced-lunch program.

Nationally, approximately 62 percent of all public elementary and secondary schools were eligible for Title I grants in 2010. About 71 percent of elementary schools received Title I funds, compared to 40 percent of middle schools and 27 percent high schools. Many districts typically distribute the funds to elementary schools, because they believe it makes more sense to address the academic problems of children when they are young. In addition, for various reasons related to peer pressure and social status, most students in secondary schools tend to shy away from the stigma of receiving a free or reduced lunch.

In 2011, the Center on Education Policy (CEP) compiled a comprehensive report regarding the achievement of Title I versus non-Title I students. Table 4 provides a snapshot of the percentages of Title I and non-Title I students scoring proficient in Grade 4 Reading for the 18 states that provided sufficient data. In all the states found in Table 4, the fourth graders in non-Title I schools outperformed their counterparts in the Title I schools. The biggest gap (-33 percentage points) between the two groups occurred in Massachusetts, and the smallest gap (-7) occurred in Tennessee. It should be noted that the differences between the states are not meaningful because each state develops its own test. Thus, the differences are due primarily to the difficulty of each state's test.

The Grade 4 Reading scores are especially important because they provide a measure of a student's future success in K–12 public education. Research consistently indicates that by third grade students transition from learning-to-read (i.e., decoding words) to reading-to-learn. The Annie E. Casey Foundation found that third graders who lack proficiency in reading are four times more likely to become high school dropouts. If this holds true, then many of the Title I fourth graders in Table 4 are at risk of dropping out of school. Moreover, on average at least 40 percent of the students in those schools come from low-income ethnic-minority families. In other words, African American and Hispanic students in Title I schools appear to be most at risk of not graduating from high school.

Table 4

Percentages of Title I and non-Title I Students Scoring Proficient on State Grade 4 Reading Tests

State	Title I Students	Non-Title I Students	Gap
Arizona	55%	74%	-19
California	42%	71%	-29
Colorado	76%	91%	-15
Delaware	80%	89%	-9
Idaho	81%	90%	-9
Kansas	80%	92%	-12
Kentucky	72%	80%	-8
Maine	49%	75%	-26
Maryland	78%	90%	-12
Massachusetts	31%	64%	-33
Missouri	35%	53%	-18
New Hampshire	56%	79%	-23
Pennsylvania	54%	81%	-27
Rhode Island	52%	78%	-26
Tennessee	88%	95%	-7
Texas	81%	93%	-12
Utah	70%	81%	-11
Washington	61%	75%	-14

In its 2011 report, the CEP also analyzed data for Grades 8 and 11. The findings for these two grades were consistent with the data for Grade 4. Essentially, there was an achievement gap between Title I and non-Title I students on their states' standardized tests. This gap, however, was not as large as the one that occurred for fourth graders. During the past decade, the achievement gaps between Title I and non-Title I students have narrowed more often than they have widened.

Researchers refer to the achievement gap between the Title I and non-Title I students as a manifestation of what is called the "Matthew Effect." This phenomenon was named after the Bible verse found in the Gospel of Matthew (13:12): *For whosoever hath, to him shall be given, and he shall have more abundance: but whosoever hath not, from him shall be taken away even that he hath.* In other words, the rich non-Title I students get richer (i.e., high gains in achievement) and the poor Title I students get poorer (i.e., small gains in achievement).

Fortunately, the Matthew Effect can be reversed through timely interventions, which is good news for school systems that want to improve the graduation rates for their high-poverty students. Unfortunately, there is some bad news, too. A large body of educational research indicates that teacher expectations can perpetuate self-fulfilling prophecies, making students more likely to succeed or fail. Teachers tend to have low expectations for poor students and those of color. When a teacher manifests this low expectation, it is often fulfilled, and the students-of-color (primarily African Americans and Hispanics) in their classroom are less likely to succeed.

In many instances, the low expectation extends beyond the teacher. It is common for districts to staff their Title I schools with inexperienced or unqualified teachers and assign their more-experienced and highly qualified teachers to non-Title I schools. This not-so-subtle form of discrimination against students from low-income families is a standard practice in many large school districts across America. Since good teaching is correlated with positive academic outcomes, many low academic outcomes for poverty-stricken students-of-color can be attributed to less-than-stellar classroom instruction. In education, good teaching matters. The term *Title I* simply indicates how poor children eat in the school's cafeteria, not how they learn in the classroom.

School Policies

Under the leadership of civil rights icons like Thurgood Marshall and Dr. King, federal laws were enacted in the twentieth century to ensure that all students regardless of their race, creed, or color had equal educational opportunities. Now that we are in the twenty-first century, several questions still linger. Do all children really have equal access to education? Have African American children truly escaped the oppressive Jim Crow laws? Have school districts discarded their racist policies? The rest of this section provides insights into these questions.

In 2014, the U.S. Education Department of Civil Rights and Data Collection released a comprehensive report regarding equal education in America. The report analyzed survey data taken from the 16,500 school districts that serve the nation's 49 million students in public education. After reviewing the report, Secretary of Education Arne Duncan stated, "It is clear that the United States has a great distance to go to meet our goal of providing opportunities for every student to succeed." The report highlights how numerous school districts in the United States continue to use their twenty-first century policies to discriminate against African American students in two major areas: discipline and access to highly qualified teachers.

The report begins with thought-provoking data related to inequities in school discipline policies. According to the report, black students were suspended or expelled at triple the rate of their white peers. Five percent of white students were suspended annually as compared to 16 percent of black students. Black girls were suspended at a rate of 12 percent, which was significantly higher than suspensions for girls in other ethnic groups.

Black students also ran a greater risk of entering the so-called "school-to-prison pipeline", which is an alarming national trend whereby children are channeled out of public schools and into the criminal justice systems.

Although blacks represented only 16 percent of all students in America's public schools, they represented 27 percent of students that were referred by schools to law enforcement. In other words, there was a greater tendency for the misbehavior of black students to be "criminalized" and "penalized" in the juvenile court system.

These outcomes are related in large part to poorly written ambiguous school policies. Too often, student discipline codes of conduct grant school administrators broad and subjective discretion to determine when a student's misbehavior warrants police involvement. For example, consider the incident that occurred at Creekside Elementary School in Milledgeville, Georgia, in 2012. In that incident, a six-year-old black girl became upset and had a tantrum in the principal's office. After this kindergartener ignored several verbal commands to calm down, which was a violation of the school's discipline code, the principal called the local police for assistance. After a police officer (who happened to be white) arrived, he promptly handcuffed the little girl and took her to the local police station.

There are so many things horribly wrong with this incident, that I don't know where to begin. For starters, children in kindergarten typically do not process verbal commands while they are in the middle of a tantrum. They need time to de-escalate, which is facilitated through the coaxing of a caring adult. When all efforts to calm the child are exhausted, then the principal should have called the parents, not the police. In this situation, the principal ignored her own common sense (i.e., call the parents) in favor of the school's explicitly biased policy (i.e., call the police).

Another eye-opening and mind-boggling incident occurred in 2016 at Graham Park Middle School in Virginia. In that incident, a school resource officer (SRO) spotted a black male student cutting line in the cafeteria and accused him of stealing a 65-cent carton of milk. When the officer put his hands on the student, the kid fidgeted and pulled away. The principal deemed the student's actions as a failure to comply with the school's policy. Consequently, the 14-year-old student was arrested, charged with petty larceny, and entered the school-to-prison pipeline by appearing in juvenile court.

In the incident at Creekside Elementary, a police officer was not on-site; the principal had to call the local police station. Graham Park Middle School, however, had its own police officer or SRO on-site ostensibly to maintain law and order. Many schools nationwide have begun to use these officers to handle routine discipline problems that were previously handled by teachers and administrators. According to a recent survey of 1,600 public schools conducted by the National Center for Education, 30 percent have an SRO on the campus. Moreover, 73 percent of schools with 1,000+ students employed one. In lieu of endeavoring to build positive relationships between students and staff, many principals use SROs to handle student discipline, thus setting the tone for the culture in their school.

The increase in the number of SROs in schools, coupled with the rise of "zero-tolerance" policies that impose suspensions for the smallest infraction, has only aggravated the problem with student discipline in our schools. Some officers receive more training than others. Too often, however, they adopt the mentality of a "beat cop" and try to perform their duties through intimidation instead of building positive relationships with students.

Undoubtedly, we cannot paint all SROs with the same broad brush because no two are the same. Frankly, during my career in public education, I observed far more positive than negative interactions between students and SROs. These officers tend to be child advocates who want to blend into a school's environment. Like anything else, problems tend to occur when their duties and responsibilities are not clearly defined in the school district's (or school principal's) policies and procedures.

Gwinnett County Public Schools (GCPS), a highly-diverse school district in Georgia with over 180,00 students and nearly 80 SROs on its payroll, is led by one of the most accomplished superintendents in the country, J. Alvin Wilbanks. However, many of its school-level administrators are notorious for using its ambiguous student discipline policy to impose harsh penalties on students for minor violations of school rules. On June19, 2017, a headline in the *Gwinnett Daily Post* publicized, "School Board hears report: Recommendations from Discipline Committee." In a decision that reeked of implicit bias, the school board either wittingly or unwittingly approved a recommendation that enabled its administrators to impose a long-term suspension (10 to 180 school days) on students who commit acts of "rude or disrespectful conduct."

Think about that for a moment. What can be more subjective than a perceived act of rudeness or disrespect, especially in a large school district with such a gaping culture gap between the students (75 percent nonwhite) and teachers (81 percent white)? From 2006 through 2016, a significant majority of out-of-school suspensions in GCPS were imposed on African American and Hispanic students for subjective infractions, such as so-called disrespectful or rude behavior. The discipline policy in GCPS has become even more discriminatory because, beginning with the 2017–2018 school year, students who commit those subjective infractions will face a hearing officer with the distinct possibility of being remanded to an alternative school for one semester (90 days) or more.

If black students are suspended from school at a disproportionate rate, are there any possible negative consequences of this? Admittedly, one could argue that there are times when out-of-school suspensions are appropriate, and I totally agree. When one student's actions pose a threat to another's health, safety, or welfare, suspensions are appropriate. However, when students are suspended for committing frivolous or subjective infractions, the absences from school could have a debilitating effect on their achievement.

With a few exceptions, most states require 180 days of instruction for students. When 10 days of suspensions are factored into the equation, many black students run the risk of receiving only 170 days (or less in many instances) of instruction each year. Research findings indicate that when students lose 10 or more days of instructional time due to suspensions, those days of instruction are difficult, if not impossible, to regain. This frequently leads to frustration, reduced achievement, and a greater probability of a student dropping out of school. These risk factors are three times greater for African American students due to the disproportionate number of suspensions that are levied on them.

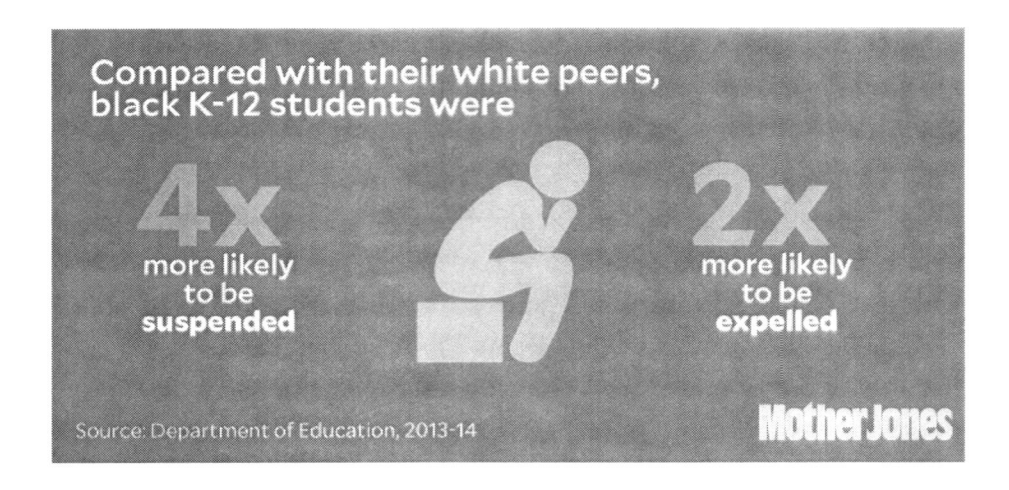

> **Compared with their white peers, black K-12 students were**
>
> **4x** more likely to be **suspended**
>
> **2x** more likely to be **expelled**
>
> Source: Department of Education, 2013-14 — MotherJones

Even when black children do manage to avoid the grip of suspensions that frequently result from the subjective interpretation of infractions outlined in the discriminatory zero-tolerance policies, they are still denied access to highly qualified teachers. According to the 2014 U.S. Data Collection report, black students are more likely than their white peers to attend schools where teachers fail to meet license and certification requirements. In addition, one in four school districts pay teachers in less-diverse high schools $5,000 less than teachers in schools with highly diverse (black and Hispanic) student populations.

The inequitable distribution of well-qualified teachers in public schools should be a major concern for all Americans, especially when we consider our ranking in education when compared to other countries in the world. The results of recent data from international math and science assessments indicate that U.S. students continue to rank near the middle of the pack and behind many other advanced industrial nations.

By virtually every measure of qualifications (i.e., certification, experience, pedagogical training, and college attended), less-qualified teachers are frequently assigned to schools that have greater numbers of low-income and minority students. Other countries with diverse populations (most notably the United Kingdom, Germany, and Canada) provide for the equal distribution of their well-qualified teachers. Consequently, their students still manage to outperform U.S. students in science, math, and reading.

In addition to having limited access to highly qualified teachers, discriminatory school policies typically inhibit African American students from having access to advanced level courses. The 2014 U.S. Data Collection report indicates that a quarter of the high schools nationwide with the highest percentage of black and Hispanic students did not offer Algebra II and a third of them did not offer chemistry. Many educators used these inequalities as evidence to support their argument for a national core curriculum in public schools.

Perhaps one of the most egregious inequities has occurred with selective enrollment in Advanced Placement (AP) courses. The College Board sponsors these courses, which offer students the opportunity to earn college credit. While blacks and Hispanics make up 37 percent of students in high school, only 27 percent were enrolled in at least one AP course and only 18 percent earned a passing score. Even though most districts are savvy enough to have written policies that do not overtly deny minority students access to AP courses, many high schools covertly encourage them to take less-challenging courses.

Most of us agree that a high school diploma can enhance a student's pursuit of the American Dream, especially for those who choose the college pathway. For many African American and Hispanic students, however, the adverse impact of biased school policies will continue to haunt them. Even when students complete high school and apply to college, residue from such biased discipline policies will continue to leave a blemish. Most colleges factor students' discipline records into their admissions decisions, especially if the disciplinary incident resulted in a written police report. Since students of color are more likely to have discipline reports that involved law enforcement officers, their college applications are at a greater risk of being rejected.

While a student's discipline record carries a substantial amount of weight on a college application, their academic record carries an even greater amount of weight. Admissions officers nationwide look for students who have challenged themselves academically and have built a stellar transcript during high school. Since black and Hispanic students are less likely to attend high schools that offer AP courses, they are less likely to meet the admissions requirements needed to matriculate in our nation's more prestigious colleges and universities. Thus, if public schools continue to implement oppressive policies that perpetuate racial discrimination, black and Hispanic students will continue their struggle to achieve the American Dream.

Teaching African American Males

African American males have made tremendous strides in education, business, and service to our country during the twenty-first century. More black men are going to college than ever before in our nation's history. The number of black-owned businesses in America has increased significantly during the past 40 years. Black men make up the largest share of people of color to serve in the U.S. Armed Forces. And on January 20, 2009, a black man, Barack H. Obama, became the 44th president of the United States.

Despite these impressive accomplishments, the media continues to broadcast a negative narrative associated with black men. They are often associated with violence, crime, poverty, and performing poorly in school. These race-based stereotypes have promulgated a sense of fear and distrust of black males. The media's portrayal of Trayvon Martin is a great example of this promulgation.

On the evening of February 26, 2012, Trayvon Martin, an unarmed 17-year-old African American student, was walking home after purchasing some candy from a local convenience store. A neighborhood watch captain, George Zimmerman, thought Trayvon "looked real suspicious" because he was black and wore a hoodie. After the watch captain confronted the teenager, a scuffle ensued and ended when Zimmerman shot and killed the unarmed teenager near his home in Sanford, Florida. This incident received national attention and sparked hot debates over racial stereotypes, gun laws, and vigilantism.

Many conservative right-wing media outlets attempted to cast Trayvon Martin's death as being justified. Following the shooting, *Fox and Friends* invited Geraldo Rivera to the show to offer his perspective of the case. He said that Trayvon was responsible for his own death because he wore a hoodie the night he was killed. Rivera asserted, "You dress like a thug, people are going to treat you like a thug. I think the hoodie is as much responsible for Trayvon Martin's death as George Zimmerman was."

The negative stereotypes of black males are still alive and well in public schools. Many administrators and teachers form their prejudice toward black students based on negative information they have heard or read. They often associate hoodies, dreads, and sagging pants with violence and gang lore. In many instances, these perceptions create feelings of discomfort for white teachers, which increases their likelihood of disengaging with black students. As previously stated, when students are engaged, they are learning; when they are disengaged, they are not learning. When they learn, they graduate.

The most informative measure of success for any public education system is its graduation rate. This metric provides clear evidence that there are huge pockets of disengagement in schools across America, especially with African American males. Since 2004, the Schott Foundation has published data in its biennial Black Boys Report series to highlight each state's progress (or lack thereof) with educating boys of color in their public schools.

Their most recent report, which was published in 2015, provided data regarding the graduation rates for black males. The report indicated that, once again, the four-year graduation rates for black males remained at the bottom in 35 of the 48 states where data was collected. Hispanic males were at the bottom in 13 states.

Most black males are enrolled in large urban districts. Therefore, an analysis of the four-year graduation rates for those school systems was conducted to gain a better understanding of outcomes for black males. Large urban districts were defined as systems with 10,000 or more black males. Table 5 provides a list of the top 10 large urban districts with the highest graduation rates for black males, and Table 6 provides the ones with the lowest rates. In both tables, graduation rates below the national averages as well as gaps above the national averages are shaded.

For the Class of 2013, the national graduation rates were 59% for black males, 65% for Hispanic males, and 80% for white males. Also, the average "graduation gap" between black males and white males was 21 percentage points. As indicated in Table 5, only four of the nation's large urban school districts scored above the national average of 59% for black males. Those districts were Montgomery County (MD), Baltimore County (MD), Fort Bend (TX), and Cumberland (NC).

The percentages in Table 6 are alarming. The graduation rates for all males—both black and white—in those school districts were below the national average. The performance of males in the Detroit (MI) public schools was disgraceful. Only 23 percent of the black males graduated in four years, and the rate for white males was even lower at 13 percent. Clearly, large urban school districts are failing to meet the educational needs of black males.

At the state level, black males graduated at the highest rates in Maine, Idaho, Arizona, South Dakota, and New Jersey with graduation rates above 75 percent. New Jersey and Tennessee were the only two states with significant black male enrollments to have a graduation rate over 70 percent. The states with the lowest graduation rates for black males had percentages of 55 or less. Those 10 states included Georgia, Michigan, Ohio, Louisiana, Indiana, Mississippi, South Carolina, Nebraska, the District of Columbia, and Nevada.

Table 5

Highest Ranked Districts for Black Male Graduates

(Enrollment of 10,000 or more Black Males)

Rank	School District	Black Enrollment	Graduate Rate Black Males	Graduation Rate White Male	Gap Black/White
1	Montgomery Co. (MD)	16,023	69%	89%	20%
2	Baltimore County (MD)	20,836	67%	76%	9%
3	Fort Bend (TX)	10,559	64%	82%	18%
4	Cumberland Co. (NC)	12,119	61%	67%	6%
5	Guilford County (NC)	15,246	57%	80%	23%
6	Prince George's Co. (MD)	44,774	55%	58%	3%
7	Cobb County (GA)	17,112	51%	75%	24%
7	Wake County (NC)	18,570	51%	82%	31%
9	Gwinnett County (GA)	24,503	50%	63%	13%
10	Nashville-Davidson (TN)	18,254	47%	57%	10%
	NATIONAL AVERAGE	N/A	59%	80%	21%

Shaded = worse than the national average.

If black males were educationally oppressed during much of the twentieth century, they are facing an educational recession in the twenty-first century. The gains they made in public education during the1980s and 1990s appear to be fading, especially in two areas that are essential for graduation: classroom instruction and student-teacher engagement. This raises several questions that districts must answer related to the teaching and learning of African American males in their schools' classrooms. Does ethnicity play a rolef in student-teacher engagement in the classroom? Are teachers using effective teaching strategies to bridge the culture gap between them and their students?

As stated earlier, African American students often lose valuable instructional time when the teacher wants them removed from their classroom for what they perceive as disrespectful behavior. When it comes to student behavior, what's polite or rude depends on how teachers read the behavior, which is determined in large part by the teacher's race or cultural background. Recent research indicates that black and white teachers give different evaluations of black students' behavior. When a black student exhibits a nondescript behavior (e.g., being tardy to class), black teachers are much less likely than white teachers to see it as problematic or disruptive.

In his best-selling book *Good to Great*, Jim Collins states that companies must confront "the brutal facts of reality" before they can become great. If school districts in America want to become great and compete internationally, there is one brutal fact that must be addressed: African American males are underachieving because of racial anxieties in the classroom. The primary source of that racial anxiety originates from negative stereotypes and the low expectations many white teachers have regarding their black male students.

One brutal fact that many school systems either ignore or attempt to disavow is the effectiveness of black teachers. In recent years, many national studies and seminars have shown that black teachers produce better academic and behavioral outcomes for black students when compared to their white colleagues. In 2016, Johns Hopkins University published a

Table 6

Lowest Ranked Districts for Black Male Graduates

(Enrollment of 10,000 or more Black Males)

Rank	School District	Black Enrollment	Graduation Rate Black Males	Graduation Rate White Males	Gap Black/White
41	Norfolk (VA)	10,578	31%	50%	19%
42	Duval County (FL)	28,116	29%	47%	18%
42	Richmond County (GA)	11,985	29%	34%	5%
44	Chatham County (GA)	10,992	28%	44%	16%
44	New York (NY)	143,972	28%	54%	26%
44	Cleveland (OH)	14,783	28%	34%	6%
44	Pinellas County (FL)	10,251	28%	54%	26%
48	Clark County (NV)	20,185	27%	45%	18%
49	Philadelphia (PA)	41,620	26%	36%	10%
50	Detroit (MI)	31,323	23%	13%	-10%
	NATIONAL AVERAGE	N/A	59%	80%	21%

Shaded = worse than the national average.

highly thought-provoking research study titled *The Long-Run Impacts of Same-Race Teachers*. The results of that study indicated that economically disadvantaged black male students who have at least one black teacher in third, fourth, or fifth grade are significantly more likely to graduate from high school and consider attending college. Those are powerful results with far-reaching implications for public education in America.

The findings in the Johns Hopkins report are not meant to imply that black teachers are better educators. However, some research suggests that black teachers are more adept at engaging or building rapport with students of color as well as with white students. One key reason cited for black students performing better with black teachers was expectations. Unlike their white counterparts, black teachers did not tend to allow negative stereotypes and an unconscious racial bias to depress teaching and learning in their classrooms.

America cannot deny the brutal reality that nearly half of the African American males in our schools are at risk of not graduating with their class. There is much at stake as more than 80 percent of teachers in our schools are white and most of them are females. The solution to this problem lies beyond simply hiring more black teachers. They cannot single-handedly combat the low expectations and racial stereotypes that depress the graduation rates for black males in virtually every U.S. school district. Besides, white teachers are not going anywhere. They will continue to make up more than 80 percent of the teachers in our nation's schools.

Consequently, reform is needed in America's K–12 public education system. Many white teachers will need to come to grips with the brutal reality that their unconscious bias, which is stimulated by negative stereotypes and fuels racial anxieties, inhibits their willingness and ability to engage black males in the classroom learning process. Once teachers and educators accept this brutal reality, they can begin the process of becoming less racially biased and more receptive of receiving training in culturally responsive pedagogy. It will create a solution where everyone benefits— white teachers as well as the black students under their trust.

Chapter Summary

Pivotal changes occurred during the twentieth century that bolstered the educational opportunities for African Americans. Federal laws were passed to open doors that were previously closed to blacks. By the end of the century, black students had left the dilapidated walls of their so-called separate-but-equal schools and were competing with their white peers in more stimulating classrooms across the nation. Despite the reforms that occurred during the twentieth century, many black students continue to feel the sting of subtle racism in public education during the twenty-first century.

The most conspicuous demographic change that occurred during the twenty-first century was an increase in the number of minority and economically disadvantaged students in public education. The year 2014 marked the first time that the statistical majority of K–12 students in America were nonwhite. As whites began to move into the suburbs, urban schools inherited the *de facto* responsibility of educating large numbers of economically disadvantaged (Title I) children of color. Many of the Title I schools had neither the monetary nor personnel resources needed to compete academically with their non-Title I counterparts.

Instead of applying the principles of multiculturalism as an approach to embrace their growing diversity, many school districts across the country opted to use their written policies to perpetuate the disparate treatment of black students, especially males. This disparate treatment has occurred primarily through discriminatory policies that govern student discipline. Black males are often suspended for committing frivolous and subjective rule infractions, such as rude behavior or disrespectful conduct. Consequently, African American students in K–12 public education are nearly four times more likely to receive an out-of-school suspension when compared to white students who commit the same subjective infraction.

The most debilitating impact of out-of-school suspensions is the removal of students from the educational process. Black males are especially at risk of losing valuable classroom instruction due to excessive suspensions. The direct impact of this can be measured in terms of graduation rates. The graduation rate for black males in America's public education system is 59 percent as compare to 80 percent for white males.

Negative stereotypes and racial anxieties continue to fuel the low expectations white teachers harbor for students of color, especially for African American males. Over 80 percent of the teachers in public education are white and middle class, which has created a culture-gap between them and their economically disadvantaged students. This culture-gap, along with white teachers' low expectations and racial biases, has had a direct impact on the low outcomes for students of color.

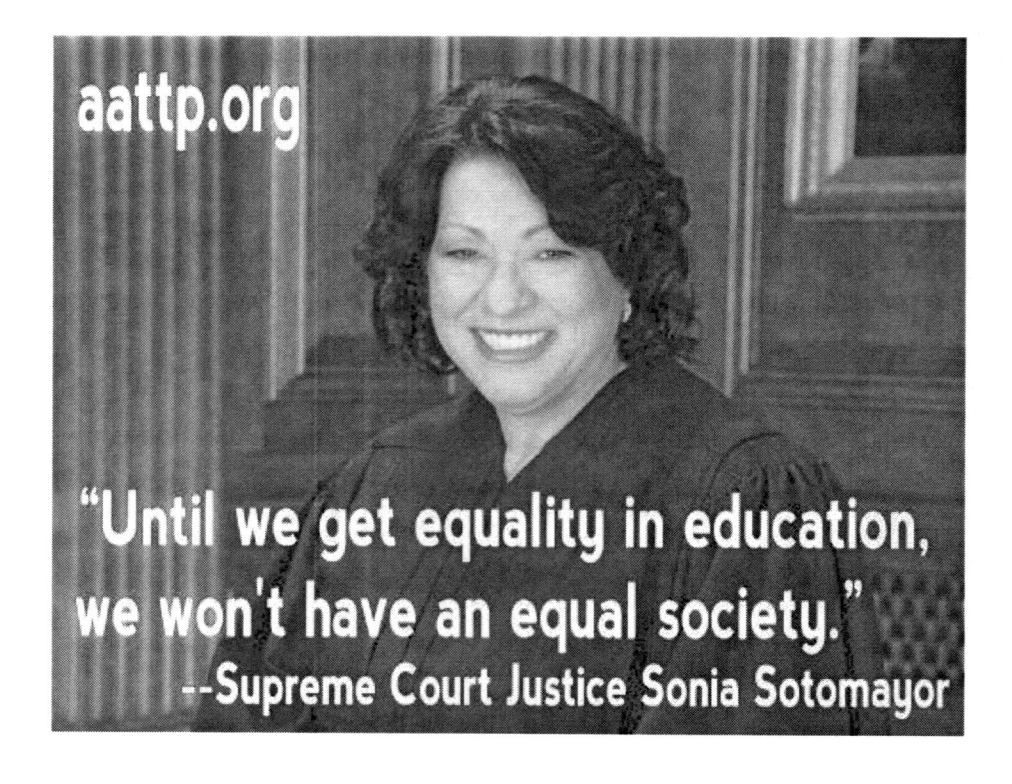

"Until we get equality in education, we won't have an equal society."
--Supreme Court Justice Sonia Sotomayor

Although it won't be easy, there is good news for public education in America. Research indicates that when compared to their white colleagues, African American teachers are more adept at engaging all students regardless of their ethnicity in classroom instruction. The negative impact of low expectations that many white teachers have for black students can, indeed, be reversed. They can be trained in the principles of multicultural education, and school board policies can be rewritten to eliminate the hidden biases of all their employees. Rhetoric, however, will not get the job done. Until (and unless) state and local school governments take decisive action, education inequality will continue to exist in our nation's public schools.

CHAPTER 6

Current Challenges in Higher Education

The latter part of the twentieth century was a golden age for black enrollment in college. Many of them took advantage of federal student loans and the recruitment efforts of predominantly white colleges to have a more inclusive and diverse student population. Black students thrived during that period and many graduated with four-year degrees that created many opportunities for them. However, things began to change at the onset of the twenty-first century. Although the enrollment of blacks in higher education has remained relatively high, their graduation rates began to decline.

Recent reports in 2017 indicate that, on average, white and Asian students earn a college-level credential at a rate about 20 percentage points higher than black and Hispanic students do. This dynamic is similar to the one in public education. In public education, black students are often denied access to advanced placement courses, and the graduation rate gap between African American and white students is about 20 percentage points. In higher education, blacks are often denied enrollment into top-tier institutions, and the graduation gap between African American and white students is almost identical.

In this chapter, we examine some of the national challenges in higher education that impact African Americans in the twenty-first century. College readiness and affordability have had more of an adverse impact on the success of economically disadvantaged students than those in other subgroups. Despite many challenges of their own, the current role of historically black colleges and universities (HBCUs) is becoming more important. Higher education remains a viable pathway to the elusive America Dream and many students of color continue to choose it.

Although college enrollment for African American students has increased from 11.7 percent in 1995 to 14.5 percent in 2014, the racial gap between African American and white students who complete college is substantially large. As with many gaps in higher education, the origin can be traced back to problems in public education. The historical context in which African Americans have received limited support for formal education has greatly contributed to this racial divide. As discussed previously, many problems in predominantly black K–12 public school settings include weak college preparatory curricula, unqualified teachers, low teacher expectations, limited access to and success in advanced placement courses, ineffective guidance counselor services, and race-based student discipline policies.

These issues have created a quagmire for many black students who complete high school with aspirations of pursuing a post-secondary education. Many prestigious colleges and universities rely heavily on standardized tests such as the SAT or ACT as part of their admissions criteria. This can be problematic for many African American students who attend high schools that do not adequately prepare them for the rigors of a four-year higher education program.

Community Colleges

Community colleges provide a viable alternative for disadvantaged African American students who are not prepared for the rigors of a four-year college. These two-year colleges were designed to address a wide variety of problems in higher education from cost and inclusivity to college and career preparedness. Most of these colleges have open enrollment, which means that any high school graduate can attend. Students can earn short-term certificates or associate degrees that prepare them for specific occupations, and tuition is usually more affordable. Many community colleges also have agreements with four-year colleges that enable students to transfer their credits.

President Obama recognized the importance of community colleges in America. In 2015, he launched his American College Promise program.

This plan made two years of community college education available and free of charge to anyone who wanted it. This proposal directed national attention to the student debt crisis in America and the need for public education to do a better job of preparing disadvantaged students for college or careers in technology.

While there are over 1,462 community colleges across America, enrollment in these two-year public institutions is declining. According to the National Student Clearinghouse Research Center, enrollment fell from 6.3 million in 2013 to 5.9 million in 2015. This represents a 7.4 percent decline during that period. The data also revealed that black students were not taking full advantage of the opportunities these institutions offered. Only 16 percent of students enrolled in community colleges were African Americans, as compared to 22 percent Hispanic, 49 percent white, 5 percent Asian, and 10 percent other.

As stated, the primary intent of community colleges is to serve as a gateway to careers or four-year colleges that offer bachelor's degrees. Unfortunately, the graduation rates for these institutions are very low. Less than 20 percent of full-time students seeking a degree get one within three years. Despite the small class sizes and more personalized instruction, many students, especially black males, arrive on the campuses woefully underprepared academically. Most of the academic deficits appear in at least one of three core high school subjects: English, math, and science. Even at the community college level, many African American students need to complete remedial or developmental courses to enhance their chances of success.

Inexplicably, many high schools across America do a poor job of touting the value of community colleges. Many high schools appear to steer their graduates to four-year institutions ostensibly to use as a talking-point to laud the excellence in their academic programs. For many high schools, having 50 of their graduates enrolled in a four-year college provides better talking-points than having 40 of their graduates enrolled in a four-year college and 10 in a two-year college. Sadly, more focus is placed on enrollment than graduation. While community colleges must improve their curriculum and instruction, high schools must do a better job of steering their most academically unprepared students into the direction of a two-year college.

Developmental Education

It could be argued that America is a place where individuals have access to success based on their race and/or socioeconomic status. In an all-too-common story, many economically disadvantaged African American students find themselves trapped in public schools with the least amount of resources and limited access to rigorous academic courses that adequately prepare them for college. It has placed many of them in what I call the "school-to-remediation" pipeline. When many low-income African American students leave high school and enter post-secondary education, colleges and universities usually funnel them into remedial classes to "fix" their academic deficiencies before they are permitted to take regular courses for credit.

While more national attention has been given to the plight of African American students in K–12 public education, their struggles in higher education during the twenty-first century have been just as challenging. Research findings in 2016 for African Americans indicate that only 9 percent attend top public research universities, 40 percent attend four-year regional colleges, and 51 percent attend community or technical colleges. Unfortunately, many low-income African American students begin their college journeys in the so-called remediation pipeline, which is more commonly referred to as *developmental education.*

Developmental education (DE), or remedial education, refers to the pre-college courses that are intended to prepare students for entry into college-level classes. More than half of African American high school graduates are deemed unprepared for college-level instruction. However, they typically are granted enrollment contingent upon the successful completion of DE courses. Once a DE curriculum is deemed necessary, students are expected to pay for a series of expensive DE courses, as many as two or three depending on the institution.

For many African American students, DE courses are viewed as an "unwanted-but-necessary-evil" they must conquer at the beginning of their college odyssey. DE courses are unwanted because they impose additional financial burdens on students who, for the most part, come from low-income families. However, these courses are a necessary evil because students must master them before they are granted full acceptance into the institution. A comprehensive study that was conducted in Ohio provides a breakdown of the relationship between a family's income range and the likelihood of being placed in a DE class. (See Table 7.)

Table 7

Percentage of Students in Developmental Education Classes by Family Income

(Ohio Public Colleges and Universities)

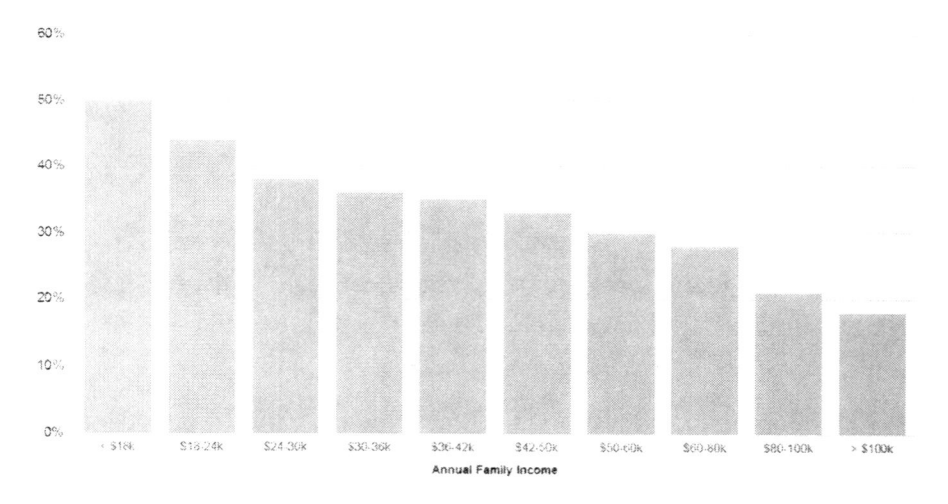

Source: Data collected and analyzed by Eric Bettinger and Bridget Long. Published in Economic Inequality and Public Education.

As indicated in Table 7, a student's likelihood of being placed in DE classes is correlated with family income. During a five-year period, 50 percent of students who attended public colleges or universities in Ohio came from families with incomes under $18,000 a year. Conversely, only 18 percent of those with family incomes over $100,000 ended up in remediation. While these results may only apply to students who were enrolled in public colleges and universities in Ohio, they provide evidence of a positive correlation between family income and a student's preparedness for college-level instruction. The trend is undeniable. In both K–12 public and higher education, students from low-income families do not perform as well academically as their counterparts from high-income families.

Many students of color are disproportionately enrolled in DE classes in colleges and universities across the country. According to national data, more than 70 percent of African American students who enroll in two-year institutions take at least one DE course. At four-year institutions, African American students are almost twice as likely to enroll in DE courses than all students combined. Moreover, African American students are more likely to need DE courses in both English and Math. In comparison to other racial or ethnic groups, black students are more likely to be required to complete DE courses in both two-year and four-year institutions.

Although African Americans comprise a large percentage of students who enroll in DE, the same is not true for teachers that provide instruction in those courses. Nearly 80 percent of the instructors are white and less than 10 percent are black. Research consistently indicates that the lack of diversity on a faculty is not beneficial to African American students. It has been documented that faculty members of color offer a broader range of instructional techniques, and they have more frequent interactions with students than white instructors.

Overall, the quality of most instructors who teach DE is less than stellar. This is the same scenario for teachers that teach in low-performing schools in large urban districts. Approximately three quarters of the DE instructors teach part-time, and many usually are not required to have any teaching experience and only a master's degree. While DE faculty positions vary by institution, they are largely composed of part-time, inexperienced, and/or adjunct faculty. One could argue that the instructors are just as unprepared as the students they teach.

Given these factors, it should come as no surprise that outcomes for students in DE programs are not as good as expected. As previously stated, a DE (or remedial) course bears no credit and must be completed before a student can enroll in a credit-bearing course. The first credit-bearing courses DE students are permitted to take are referred to as gateway courses. These typically are basic freshman-level English, math, history, and science courses.

The success of students who begin in DE and proceed to a gateway (i.e., credit-bearing) course is very low. Only 20 percent of students who enroll in a DE math class make the transition to a gateway class, and only 37 percent of students enrolled in a DE English course move forward. As for the many African American students who require developmental education, very few of them complete gateway courses within two years. In other words, they seldom get on track to earn the credits needed to earn a college degree.

When students enroll in DE programs, they are required to either take (a) both English and math, (b) English only, or (c) math only. For whatever reason, African American students in four-year institutions have better success with DE courses than their counterparts in two-year institutions. At two-year institutions, after completing both developmental math and English, only 7 percent of African Americans move forward to successfully complete both gateway math and English courses. On the contrary, in the same scenario at four-year institutions, 17 percent of African American students move forward to successfully complete those gateway courses. The completion percentages for gateway courses for African American students in two-year and four-year institutions are presented in Table 8.

Table 8

Completion of Gateway Courses for

African American Students at Two-Year and Four-Year Institutions

Gateway Course	Four-Year Institutions	Two-Year Institutions	Difference
Math and English	17%	7%	-10
English only	39%	22%	-17
Math only	25%	14%	-11

Data source: 2016 Complete College America report.

As indicated in Table 8, African American students in four-year institutions complete gateway courses at a higher rate of success when compared to their counterparts in two-year institutions. There are two far-reaching ramifications of these findings, and both are related to teaching strategies for black students.

First, the data in Table 8 should redirect attention back to the challenges that public schools face with teaching and preparing black students for the rigors of post-secondary education. Second, attention should also now be directed at the teaching that occurs in DE classes. Evidence suggests that, just like in K–12 public education, ineffective instructors have difficulty improving outcomes for low-income African American students. In all classroom situations, good teaching matters!

The importance of good teaching in K–12 public education cannot be overstated. Far too many students of color are graduating without being ready for college. Grade inflation plays a substantial role in masking the academic deficiencies these students have. Evidence suggests that principals often encourage their teachers to give unearned passing grades to students of color to improve the school district's graduation rate. As educators continue their efforts to raise the college graduation rates for students of color, more attention must be focused on improving the quality of instruction in DE classes.

Historically Black Colleges and Universities

Historically black colleges and universities (HBCUs) were created in America during a time when racism was explicit and educating blacks was neither a priority nor encouraged. Throughout the twentieth century, HBCUs played a pivotal role in transforming the landscape of higher education in America by providing opportunities for black students to attend college. Until the mid-1960s, HBCUs were, with very few exceptions, the only higher education option for most African Americans. By the early-1990s, these institutions became more racially and ethnically diverse as a greater number of Hispanics began to enroll, especially in regions of the country where that population was growing rapidly.

Today, there are 105 HBCUs in 19 states plus the District of Columbia and the U.S. Virgin Islands. Although HBCUs enroll 11 percent of African American students in the United States, they represent less than 3 percent of all colleges and universities in the country. These institutions are public and private, religious and nonsectarian, two-year and four-year, and urban and rural. HBCUs reflect the variety that we have in higher education in the United States.

While HBCUs thrived during the twentieth century, they currently appear to have entered into a state of flux. In addition to a decline in enrollment, their graduation rates have fallen, too. In 2016, the average graduation rate at a four-year HBCU was approximately 59 percent. Although this figure was higher than the national average for African American students at non-HBCUs, no HBCU had a graduation rate above 70 percent. Spelman College in Atlanta had the highest at 69 percent, followed by Howard University in Washington, D.C., with 65 percent. The graduation rates for more than half of the HBCUs were below 34 percent.

By comparison, the graduation rates for African American students at prestigious institutions such as Harvard (MA), Amherst College (MA), Swarthmore (PA), Yale (CT), and Princeton (NJ) were above 90 percent. These institutions are considered prestigious because they typically accept less than 7 percent of all students that apply for admissions. Therefore, it is obvious that these schools accept only the crème-de-la-crème of African American students who have a high-probability of graduating. Nevertheless, in the spirit of the Statue of Liberty, the mantra of HBCUs has always been "give me your tired, your poor, your huddled masses...".

Perhaps the greatest challenge to HBCUs in the twenty-first century is underfunding. Declining enrollment has had a debilitating effect on university funds. A recent study indicates that HBCU alumni are less likely to donate to their alma mater for a variety of personal reasons. In addition, HBCUs do not receive nearly as much government money as compared to non-HBCUs. Congress also made a drastic reduction in the length or terms of Pell grants, which slashed a significant amount of funds previously available to low-income students. These cuts to the Pell Grants have had a huge financial impact on HBCUs because many of their students depend on those funds to offset rising tuition costs.

While the poor HBCUs have struggled financially, the rich non-HBCUs have continued to prosper. For example, statistics show that Brown University receives $3.2 billion in government funding, which is less than any other Ivy League institution. By comparison, Howard University—the "richest" of the HBCUs—receives a nominal $586.1 million. The lack of funding forces many institutions to cut costs, eliminate programs, and sell valuable resources. During the past decade, the cumulative effects of having to make programmatic and operational cuts have made HBCUs less attractive to incoming students.

Economic factors notwithstanding, societal factors have also contributed to the demise of many HBCUs. Many Americans live in what can be described as a "post-racial society" or a society in which the significance of race is rapidly declining. Thus, when black high school graduates can choose between a potentially struggling HBCU or an Ivy League institution, many will choose the latter. President Barack Obama, however, made it clear that we are not living in a post-racial era in America. During his commencement address to about 2,300 Howard University graduates on May 7, 2016, the then-president encouraged them to embrace their blackness and added that "my election did not create a post-racial society."

Given the circumstances related to social, financial, and academic challenges, many HBCUs across the nation struggle to reclaim their positive image as well as their viability. Some, however, have already lost their struggle. St. Paul's College in Virginia, for example, was forced to close its doors in 2013 due to a lack of financial stability. Morris Brown College in Atlanta lost its accreditation in 2002 and had less than 40 students enrolled in 2015. In addition, some university presidents have come under fire for misusing funds. This elicits the question, are HBCUs still relevant today?

America's higher education system is more diverse today than at any point in its history. This trend has altered the makeup of many colleges and universities nationwide. In slightly more than one quarter of the HBCUs across the nation, at least 20 percent of the student body is non-black. Some people worry that the changing composition of HBCUs jeopardizes the very aspects that make them unique. Others argue that diversity makes these institutions stronger and offers an opportunity for the broader population to appreciate the black culture. The latter argument makes a strong case for inclusion.

Even though the majority of African American college students are enrolled at predominantly white institutions, HBCUs are not becoming less black. In fact, they remain the top producers of black graduates in many disciplines. HBCUs can produce these results due to their explicit commitment to educating black students in nurturing, supportive environments. Unfortunately, some state and federal policymakers fail to grasp the significance of these factors that foster teaching and learning in HBCUs. For example, in 2014, North Carolina legislators proposed shutting down Elizabeth City State University (ECSU) because it was "small and unprofitable." Ironically, ECSU's graduation rate ranked near the top among all HBCUs. That university is still open today, and its students are performing nicely.

HBCUs have been widely criticized for having a graduation rate that hovers on average around 30 percent. While this figure may appear highly unfavorable, it does not tell the full story. In many ways, HBCUs are like Title I schools in public education. Both entities serve many economically disadvantaged students. When considering graduation rates, it is important to keep in mind that a significant number of low-income (Pell-Grant-eligible), first-generation college students with low SAT scores are enrolled in HBCUs. Research indicates that students with this profile are less likely to graduate no matter where they attend college. Table 9 provides a breakdown of the percentage of students at each HBCU that receive a Pell Grant.

There can be little argument that HBCUs do, indeed, accept America's "tired, poor, and huddled masses" into their fold. Despite the progress that has been made against racism in America, it is important to remember that the fight for civil rights and equality still rages on. Contrary to a popular belief, America is not a nonracial society. HBCUs are keenly aware of past and present struggles, and they accept students who never tire of learning in an educational environment that embraces the rich heritage of African Americans. While on campus, students receive a constant reminder as to why HBCUs were developed and the role they played in the Civil Rights movement by producing such icons as Martin Luther King Jr. (Morehouse College) and Thurgood Marshall (Lincoln University and Howard University).

As evidenced in Table 9, HBCUs open their doors to many poor students by making college affordable. As college costs climb, HBCUs remain reasonable options for earning college degrees and offer many opportunities for financial aid through grants, scholarships, and federal loans. HBCUs like Coahoma Community College in Clarksdale, Mississippi, cost as little as $4,940 for in-state students for an entire academic year. These costs are lowered even more when any financial aid is deducted from the total. Financial aid programs at HBCUs have a keen understanding that many of their students come from homes where college may not be an option without assistance. Invariably, they step up to meet the financial needs of those students.

HBCUs continue to welcome the huddled masses of students that other predominantly white colleges do not want. They open their doors to people who have experienced all forms of social, cultural, economic, academic, racial, and political oppression. For example, they have taken bold steps toward advancing rights for lesbian, gay, bisexual, and transgender (LGBT) students. Rather than simply giving lip service to controversial or sensitive issues, Morehouse College recently acted by offering its first LBGT course.

Yes, HBCUs are still relevant today. These institutions are credited with having created the American black middle class, and graduates continue to provide invaluable service to all Americans. According to a report by the U.S. Commission on Civil Rights, HBCUs have produced the following:

- 40% of African American members of Congress
- 40% of African American engineers
- 50% of African American professors at predominantly white institutions
- 50% of African American lawyers
- 80% of African American judges

Table 9
Percentage Pell Grant Recipients at HBCUs

Large Majorities of Students at Almost All of the Nation's Black Colleges and Universities Are From Low-Income Families

Two thirds of students at a majority of the black colleges receive federal Pell Grants, which are reserved for low-income students.

Black College or University	Total Students	Pell Grant Recipients	% of All Students Who Get Pell Grants
Livingstone College	907	892	98.3 %
Lane College	1,370	1,322	96.5
Southern Univ.-New Orleans	1,719	1,652	96.1
Morris College	824	786	95.4
Mississippi Valley State Univ.	2,686	2,501	93.1
Miles College	1,738	1,558	89.6
Benedict College	2,531	2,257	89.2
Jarvis Christian College	675	596	88.3
Texas College	733	636	86.8
Southern Univ.-Shreveport	2,387	1,973	82.7
Voorhees College	710	586	82.5
Allen University	530	435	82.1
Philander Smith College	580	474	81.7
Edward Waters College	842	684	81.2
Paul Quinn College	784	629	80.2
Alcorn State University	3,015	2,341	77.6
Jackson State University	6,523	5,053	77.5
Alabama State University	4,584	3,526	76.9
Stillman College	815	625	76.7
Cheyney Univ. of Pennsylvania	1,494	1,130	75.6
St. Augustine's College	1,247	939	75.3
Grambling State University	4,584	3,449	75.2
LeMoyne-Owen College	714	537	75.2
Central State University	1,747	1,309	74.9
Southwestern Christian College	202	151	74.8
Rust College	920	688	74.8
Tougaloo College	913	675	73.9
Florida Memorial University	1,784	1,309	73.4
Claflin University	1,674	1,224	73.1
Texas Southern University	9,053	6,554	72.4
Shaw University	2,669	1,926	72.2
Paine College	913	656	71.9
Univ. of Arkansas-Pine Bluff	3,051	2,191	71.8
Wiley College	862	619	71.8
Dillard University	1,124	806	71.7
Saint Paul's College	681	486	71.4
South Carolina State Univ.	3,839	2,742	71.4
Langston University	2,557	1,818	71.1
Albany State University	3,515	2,482	70.6
Fort Valley State University	2,086	1,471	70.5
Harris-Stowe State College	1,868	1,317	70.5 %
Southern Univ.-Baton Rouge	7,335	5,145	70.1
Alabama A&M University	4,978	3,477	69.8
Huston-Tillotson College	705	485	68.8
Bethune-Cookman University	3,093	2,117	68.4
Wilberforce University	858	583	67.9
Coppin State University	3,310	2,244	67.8
Savannah State University	3,109	2,042	65.7
Elizabeth City State Univ.	2,620	1,721	65.7
Johnson C. Smith University	1,470	963	65.5
Lincoln University (Penn.)	1,860	1,190	64.0
Fayetteville State University	5,399	3,442	63.8
Florida A&M University	10,124	6,463	63.8
Bennett College	607	383	63.1
Talladega College	425	251	59.1
Xavier University	2,272	1,338	58.9
Clark Atlanta University	3,681	2,134	58.0
Virginia State University	4,306	2,474	57.5
Winston-Salem State Univ.	5,329	3,021	56.7
Prairie View A&M Univ.	5,813	3,272	56.3
North Carolina Central Univ.	6,614	3,578	54.1
Tennessee State University	7,112	3,762	52.9
Kentucky State University	2,339	1,230	52.6
Tuskegee University	2,420	1,236	51.1
Norfolk State University	5,403	2,874	53.2
Virginia Union University	1,238	631	51.0
N. Carolina A&T State Univ.	9,687	4,684	48.4
Morgan State University	5,955	2,879	48.3
Delaware State University	3,303	1,577	47.7
Lincoln University (Missouri)	2,927	1,334	45.6
Univ. of Md. Eastern Shore	3,697	1,677	45.4
Fisk University	901	405	45.0
Oakwood College	1,771	750	42.3
Hampton University	5,135	2,107	41.0
Spelman College	2,290	890	38.9
Bowie State University	4,075	1,455	35.7
Morehouse College	2,933	1,042	35.5
Univ. of District of Columbia	5,300	1,851	34.9
Howard University	7,309	2,375	32.5

Source: U.S. Department of Education.

Student Debt and the American Dream

There is no universal definition for the proverbial American Dream—it references different things to different people at different times. During the Civil War, African Americans were considered property in Southern states. Their American Dream was to obtain freedom, flee the oppression of Jim Crow laws, build a cabin home, and secure a plot of land to grow crops and raise small livestock.

The American Dream for many African Americans shifted during the years after World War II. Although they had enjoyed over 80 years of legal freedom, many of their civil rights were denied due to societal racism. Thus, their dream was to have equality (or equal treatment) in areas such as education, employment, public accommodations, voting, and housing. This dream was realized through the Civil Rights Act of 1964.

In 2014, First Lady Michelle Obama outlined the pathway to the American Dream when she addressed a crowd of African American students at Booker T. Washington High School in Atlanta. "Do you hear what I'm telling you?" she asked the teenagers. "Because I'm giving you some insights that a lot of rich kids all over the country—they know this stuff, and I want you to know it, too. Because you have got to go and get your education. You've got to." Mrs. Obama's message was a blueprint of the pathway to the American Dream for young African Americans—*Do not drop out of school. Go to college. Get out of poverty. Giving up on education is not an option.*

Previously, we discussed how college has become more affordable for low-income students. Student loans and other forms of financial aid have served to reduce students' stress while they are pursuing their college degrees. However, this stress intensifies substantially after graduation. Higher education has long been considered the primary way to escape poverty, but it comes with a cost which is presented in the form of student loan debt. For African American students, this cost is often greater for them than for their white colleagues, and the burden to repay their student loans often follows them for decades after graduation.

Even the Obamas candidly acknowledged the fact that loans were used to help finance their education and paved the way for them to attend prestigious universities. The Obamas further acknowledged that it took years for them to repay these loans. In their statements to audiences across the nation, they expressed sympathy to students who are shackled with rising tuition costs and the stressful burden that follows with having to repay student loans.

The costs for higher education are skyrocketing. The average cost for four years of tuition and housing is nearly $44,000 at private colleges and approximately $20,000 at public colleges. When the average college graduate in the class of 2016 walked across the stage during the commencement ceremony, he or she exited with a degree and $37,172 in debt, a 6 percent increase in student loan debt from 2015.

For African American students, especially those from low- to moderate-income families, the struggle to repay student debt is greater. They are twice as likely to borrow for college as their white counterparts. Based on a study conducted by the Brookings Institution, the student debt for blacks averaged over $27,000 as compared to a little under $20,00 for white students. Asian and Hispanic students had even less debt than whites. Table 10 provides a breakdown of race and student debt.

Table 10

Race and Student Debt

(Estimated Education Debt by Race)

Group	White	Black	Asian	Hispanic	Other
Student Debt	$19,695	$27,416	$18,267	$17,618	$21,735

Data Source: Grinstein-Weiss, Perantie, Taylor, Guo, and Raghavan (2016).

Approximately 63 percent of white students who graduate from public four-year colleges and universities borrow money to do so, as compared to 81 percent of African American graduates. As for two-year colleges, 57 percent of African American students borrow money in comparison to 43 percent of whites. In addition, African American students on average borrow $2,000 more to finance their costs for a two-year college program.

The American Dream for African Americans in the twenty-first century is virtually the same dream as for everyone else. They want to be gainfully employed, own a home, and maintain the fundamental rights of all U.S. citizens (i.e., the right to practice religion, equal protection of laws, and the freedom of speech). African Americans realize that a college education increases their chances of having access to the first two components of the dream—being employed and owning a home. Once students enter higher education, however, there is no guarantee that their American Dream will come to fruition (either with or without a degree) because student debt can disrupt their plans.

Despite receiving financial aid, many students drop out of school before earning their degree. This is especially true for students of color. When asked, around 69 percent of African American college students stated that debt was the primary reason for dropping out. Forty-three percent of white college dropouts cited the same reason. Student loan debt and the increasing cost of higher education are two issues that have a profound impact on younger generations who are eager to gain financial traction. These factors push the younger generation farther away from the American Dream of being gainfully employed and owning a home, especially for young African American citizens.

Despite years of efforts at the federal, state, and local levels, racial disparities or gaps continue to persist across America. These gaps have included the black-white achievement gap, the black-white secondary education graduation gap, the black-white higher education graduation gap, the student-teacher culture gap, and the black-white student debt gap. Invariably, each gap is characterized by white students having a competitive advantage over their nonwhite counterparts. The employment gap between black and white college graduates also is another gap that impacts the American Dream.

Although college attendance for minorities has increased in recent years, workers at all levels still find employment disparities. According to a report compiled by the Economic Policy Institute, the average unemployment rate for blacks who graduated from a four-year college hovered around 4.1 percent during 2016. This was nearly twice the unemployment rate for whites with a four-year college degree (2.4 percent) and equivalent to the unemployment rate for whites with an associate's or two-year degree. In essence, black workers must attain more education to earn the same amount of money as less qualified white employees.

While the numbers for college degrees are alarming, the employment gap widens significantly when black and white workers without a high school diploma are compared. At that level, unemployment for whites is 6.9 percent and 16.6 percent for blacks. The words of Michelle Obama ring true, "(blacks) have got to go and get (their) education" as these figures provide clear evidence that increased education does, indeed, bring unemployment rates closer for both ethnic groups.

For decades, institutions of higher education had not taken an active role in preparing their graduates for the working world. Graduates tended to fade off into the sunset once they received their degrees, as they're often ill-prepared to face the challenges that waited for them. Fortunately, many colleges and universities are focusing on providing career advisement to increase employment opportunities for their students following graduation. These advisement programs emphasize the importance of networking and building social connections as crucial factors for finding jobs. Participation in advisement and networking programs may be a tool to rectify some of the employment imbalance for minority students.

The American Dream is being pushed further out of reach for younger generations. Many economists believe that in the twenty-first century, the dream is more accessible in our neighboring country to the north, Canada. There seems to be no shortage of explanations. Factors such as inflation and wage discrimination against minorities (i.e., blacks, Hispanics, and women) in the business sector pose ongoing challenges. Although a college degree can lead to the elusive dream, student loan debt can create barriers along the way, especially for young African Americans.

Chapter Summary

As the price of college has skyrocketed and tens of thousands of recent graduates have found themselves either unemployed or stuck in jobs that do not require a degree, higher education has come under scrutiny for its apparent failure to make students job-ready. There seems to be a disconnect between what employers want out of today's college graduates and what schools are producing. One is compelled to ask, what is the purpose of higher education?

The larger purpose of higher education, beyond preparation for employment, is to connect students with real-world problems and get them engaged in creative problem-solving. This has created significant challenges in higher education because many students graduate from high school with glaring academic deficiencies. While two-year colleges offer a more specialized curriculum focusing on workforce training, four-year colleges offer a broader curriculum requiring critical thinking in a variety of subject areas.

Regardless of the setting—two-year or four-year college—many students must complete some sort of developmental education (DE) or remediation courses before they can pursue coursework for their degree. Students must pay additional tuition to take these DE courses, and they do not earn any credit for taking them. A significant number of low-income African American students are required to take at least one DE course and over 50 percent fail them. Consequently, they never gain full-admission status and drop out of school.

Despite ongoing economic challenges, many HBCUs remain viable options for many low-income African American students. These institutions have also attracted students from other ethnic groups, as roughly a quarter of the HBCUs across America have at least a 20 percent non-African American student body. These black institutions of higher education remain relevant in the twenty-first century because they provide safe and nurturing learning environments for many low-income students who would be at-risk of failing in a non-HBCU setting.

In the twenty-first century, the American Dream is to become gainfully employed and own a home. For many Americans, the path to that dream runs through college campuses. A college degree significantly improves a person's chances of obtaining that dream. Unfortunately, accumulated student loan debt can derail a person's access to that dream. This is especially true for African Americans as 81 percent of them graduate with student loan debt. Moreover, many African American graduates encounter wage discrimination, which further hinders their ability to repay their student loans.

One of the greatest challenges for America's education system is to bridge the gap between secondary and higher education, especially for educating low-income and disadvantaged students. Too many black and Hispanic students graduate from high school with substantial academic deficiencies. This issue can be mitigated by including more college prep courses in high school and hiring more teachers of color to teach them.

This same strategy can also be used once students enter higher education. Undoubtedly, some (hopefully not as many) African American students will continue to need access to some developmental education courses. Given the importance of these courses for minority students to gain full-admission status, colleges and universities should hire more highly qualified instructors to teach them. Whenever possible, African American instructors should teach the remedial courses because, according to research, they are more adept at engaging minority students in classroom learning.

In summary, the challenges that confront higher education in the twenty-first century can be obtained through changes in policies related to issues that are captured in the acronym FAIR—*funding, affordable, instructors*, and *relevant*. Legislators should lobby for additional funding to support the HBCUs in their respective states. Federal, state, and local governmental officials should explore ways to make college more affordable for all students.

Institutions of higher education should hire more highly qualified instructors, especially to teach their developmental education courses. Finally, colleges and universities should fine-tune the components of their written academic programs to ensure that they are relevant and adequately prepare students for the job market.

PART III

STRATEGIES FOR TWENTY-FIRST CENTURY REFORM IN EDUCATION

CHAPTER 7

Higher Education— Reform Actions Needed

Throughout the past century, virtually the same factors have impacted students in both public and higher education. Those factors have included the 3 Ps—*policy and governance*, *poverty*, and *personnel* and *instruction*. Until and unless these factors are addressed, no substantive or meaningful changes can occur in our educational system. In the next two chapters, I will offer reforms that are needed to address these issues thus, creating a renaissance for K–12 public and higher education in America.

Policy and Governance

Issues related to policies in higher education can run the gamut from admissions criteria to guidelines for guns on campus. Although the federal government has a department of education, public institutions of higher education operate under the control of their state's government. Under the current secretary of education, Betsy DeVos, there is a move toward eliminating federal involvement in higher education. Nevertheless, there are policies that can be implemented at the state and federal levels to reform and improve higher education in America. These policies should focus on making reforms in four areas: funding, academic freedom and civil rights, student management, and safe campus environments.

Funding

Most public universities in the United States rely heavily on private funding sources such as tuition payments and gains on endowment assets. Still, the federal government allocates billions of dollars annually to thousands of universities in the form of research and development grants and contracts, as well as financial aid to undergraduates through the Federal Pell Grant Program. Historically, the more prestigious institutions have received the greatest amount of funding from the federal government. Table 11 provides a list of the top 20 institutions that have received the most funding from the federal government in 2016.

Table 11

Institutions Receiving the Most

Funding from the Federal Government in 2016

Rank	Institution	Amount
1	Johns Hopkins	$2.0 Billion
2	University of Washington	$960.6 Million
3	University of Michigan	$756.1 Million
4	Stanford University	$679.6 Million
5	University of California, San Diego	$643.0 Million
6	University of Pennsylvania	$617.0 Million
7	Columbia University	$599.9 Million
8	Pennsylvania State University	$599.8 Million
9	University of North Carolina	$599.2 Million
10	University of Pittsburgh	$580.3 Million
11	Duke University	$562.8 Million
12	Georgia Institute of Technology	$562.6 Million
13	University of Wisconsin	$551.4 Million
14	Harvard University	$550.5 Million
15	University of Calif., San Francisco	$535.5 Million
16	University of Calif., Los Angeles	$535.3 Million
17	University of Minnesota	$505.3 Million
18	Massachusetts Institute of Technology	$491.4 Million
19	Ohio State University	$488.0 Million
20	Yale University	$480.2 Million

Source: 24/7 Wall Street (March 2017).

As expected, most of the institutions in Table 11 serve many students who come from upper middle-class households. These institutions provide evidence to support the axiom that in higher education "the rich get richer." For example, in addition to the $617,500,000 it received from the federal government, the University of Pennsylvania had an endowment of $10.7 billion. Moreover, the university recently purchased and renovated an old DuPont facility and converted it into a 58,000-square foot research laboratory.

The picture for HBCUs is bleak when compared to other four-year institutions in America. Nearly 90 percent of all students who attend HBCUs rely on federal grants and work study programs to finance their education. In President Donald Trump's proposed budget for the 2018 fiscal year, the administration proposed to significantly reduce the federal work study program as well as eliminate Supplemental Educational Opportunity Grants, which offer need-based aid to nearly 1.6 million low-income undergraduates each year. For HBCUs, the axiom is the opposite— "the poor get poorer."

While federal funding goes to students at public, private, and for-profit colleges, state funding goes primarily to public institutions. Historically, colleges have received far more funding from their states than from the federal government. During the past decade, states have spent 65 percent more on higher education than the federal government. Unfortunately, due to the great recession in 2010, many states had to make annual cuts in their funding for public colleges and universities. These cuts drove up the costs for tuition and impaired students' educational experiences by forcing faculty reductions, fewer course offerings, and campus closings. These factors made college less affordable and less accessible for many students who need degrees to pursue the American Dream.

While some states have begun to restore some of the deep cuts in support for their public two-year and four-year institutions since the recession, their funding remains lower than it was just prior to the recession. Essentially, costs related to funding cuts and increased tuition have shifted from the states to the students. In addition, students attending HBCUs have suffered the most since the recession.

The central issue related to policy in higher education is college affordability. It is time to renew investment in funding higher education to promote college affordability and quality. It will require action from both state and federal policymakers. At the federal level, policymakers must increase the amount of federal dollars, which are budgeted to support colleges and universities that serve students from low-income families. According to Michael Lomax, the president of the United Negro College Fund, federal cuts to federal student aid programs and the elimination of the Supplemental Educational Opportunity Grants would negatively impact the ability of more than 81,000 students in HBCUs to pay for college.

State-level policymakers should be just as vigilant as their counterparts at the federal level. Understandably, many states have had to deal with a revenue collapse, which was caused by the economic downturn that began in 2010. State lawmakers relied heavily on spending cuts to offset lost revenue. Moving forward, state legislators must make tax and budget choices that recognize the importance of investing in human capital and quality education. States must renew their commitment to a high-quality, affordable system of higher education by increasing the revenue to those institutions. This investment in higher education would help build a stronger middle class and increase the workforce of skilled workers needed during the twenty-first century in America.

Academic Freedom and Civil Rights

In our democratic society, students do not leave their civil rights outside of campus; they carry those rights with them wherever they venture in America. The same democratic principles are manifested inside the classroom in the form of academic freedom. The essence of academic freedom is the freedom of teachers, students, and academic institutions to pursue knowledge wherever it may lead without censorship or unreasonable constraint. In its basic form, academic freedom involves the freedom to engage in a multidimensional range of activities to produce knowledge. For college professors, this could encompass an approach such as choosing a research focus, determining what to teach in the classroom, presenting research findings to colleagues, and publishing research findings.

Nevertheless, academic freedom has limits. In the United States, for example, most colleges and universities require their instructors to operate under the tenets of the 1940 Statement on Academic Freedom and Tenure. Under this policy, teachers in higher education are urged carefully avoid overly controversial subject matter. Furthermore, when they speak or write in public, although they are free to express their opinions without fear of retribution from the institution, they must show restraint and clearly indicate that they are not speaking for their institution. Academic tenure protects academic freedom by ensuring that teachers can be fired only for gross misconduct or professional incompetence.

Most institutions of higher education in America have often been accused of having liberal and progressive biases. This perception reached a crescendo during the first months of Donald Trump's presidency in 2017. From Berkeley to Charlottesville, protests were staged on college campuses over appearances by those deemed "messengers of the right." Their protests varied from civil disobedience to serious violence. Proponents of the so-called extreme right (e.g., neo-Nazis, Ku Klux Klan, Aryan Nation, and Alt-Right) were denied any right to speak on American college campuses. This right-versus-left conflict has existed ever since I attended college in the mid-1960s during the Civil Rights and Vietnam War eras. Historically, on college campuses, it seems as if the "right" has been wrong, until the "left" is all that is left at college.

Campus conflicts have caused conservative policymakers in some states to question the liberal biases that many institutions appear to harbor. The stark divide between college campuses and state policymakers on socio-cultural and civil rights issues made the headlines throughout 2016. In Wisconsin, a few policymakers voiced their objections to a course offered at the University of Wisconsin-Madison titled, "The Problem of Whiteness." In Tennessee, policymakers pulled funding from the University of Tennessee's Office of Diversity and Inclusion for hosting an event called "Sex Week" as an effort to be more accommodating to the lesbian, gay, bisexual, transgender, and queer (LGBTQ) community. Finally, Missouri policymakers attempted to hold the University of Missouri accountable for a series of protests led by a Black Lives Matter group because they thought the students embarrassed the state.

Realistically, the threats made by lawmakers to withhold or pull fixed funding usually do not materialize. However, these threats are symbolic of a divide that must be bridged to make higher education a state priority. Since this divide is rooted in issues related to civil rights, the solution or bridge must be grounded in policy or federal law. As previously mentioned, students do not forfeit their civil rights while on college campuses or anywhere else in America.

The Office of Civil Rights, located in the U. S. Department of Education, enforces several federal civil rights laws which prohibit discrimination in programs or activities that receive federal funds from the Department of Education. These laws extend to all state education agencies, elementary and secondary school systems, colleges and universities, and vocational schools. Thus, the solution to the issue of academic freedom and students' civil rights must involve clear and concise policies that are grounded in federal statutes.

First, colleges must ensure that no student's civil rights are violated. Their policies must be explicitly nondiscriminatory, enable academic freedom, and be readily available for review on the college's website. Oversight of the enforcement of these policies should be assigned to an attorney in the college or university's office of student affairs.

Second, each state's governor must declare higher education a priority and work with the state's legislative body to ensure that their institutions of higher education are adequately funded. Most importantly, governors must enact or reinforce laws and policies ensuring that all students are afforded their civil rights and all institutions of higher education adhere to the tenets of the doctrine of academic freedom. These policies or reforms will foster the realization of quality higher educational opportunities for all students in America.

Student Debt Management

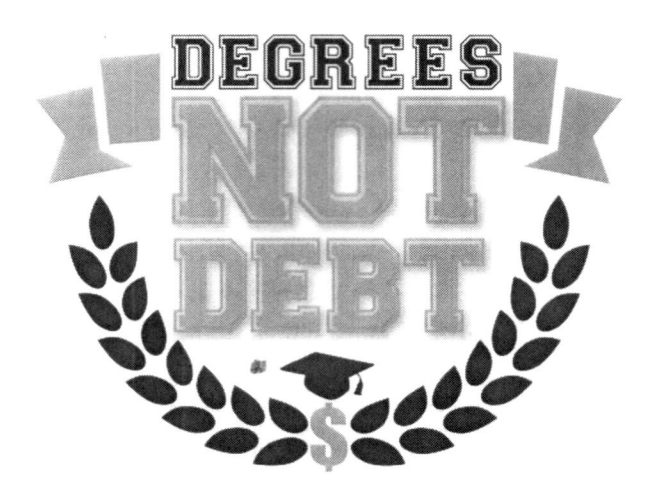

As you are aware by now, college is notoriously expensive. In March 2017, the Institute for Higher Education Policy published a report indicating that 70 percent of colleges are unaffordable for lower-income and middle-income students who are unable to obtain student loans. For the students that do manage to get financial assistance, repaying the debt has become an issue for state policymakers. More specifically, student loan refinancing and loan forgiveness are an emerging policy priority in many states.

Lawmakers are keenly aware of the need to restructure federal student loans, and they have engaged in open political discussions that have branched in many directions. While Senator Bernie Sanders proposes to make college education "free" to students, Senator Lamar Alexander favors requiring colleges and universities to bear part of the responsibility of paying students loans if the borrower defaults. The solution to the problem lies somewhere between those two perspectives. Undoubtedly, lawmakers and policymakers must work together to pass some sort of comprehensive legislation to make college more affordable and to reduce poverty-inducing student loan debts.

In 2016, policymakers in Missouri and Virginia proposed legislation that would enable students to refinance their student loans. Although similar legislation passed in seven other states, this bill did not pass in Missouri and Virginia. Policymakers in Oregon are considering policy proposals that would enable students to use their loan expenses as deductions or credits on their state taxes.

Policymakers in Nebraska and Wisconsin have taken a more proactive approach to addressing debt management by providing financial literacy to student borrowers. The policymakers in those two states have passed legislation to provide students with more information about their loans and repayment options. They also want to increase awareness of federal public service loan forgiveness programs among eligible constituents. As college debts continue to spiral out of control and strangle students, state policymakers must continue to explore policies to ease debt burdens.

Since passing legislation is somewhat of an inexact science, families should not sit idly and wait for politicians to determine the financial fate of their children's college future. One thing families can do while legislators are grappling with the problem is to invest in a 529 College Savings Plan. These state-operated plans are designed to help families set aside funds for future college costs. Many states enable savings from these plans to accrue without requiring investors to pay state taxes on the interest earned. Money can be withdrawn from the accounts tax-free and can be used for tuition, books, and other education-related expenses at most accredited two-year and four-year colleges and universities.

Policymakers and families will have to join forces to defeat this imposing Goliath known as student debt. Although Senator Sanders' idea of "tuition-free" college is intriguing, many of his fellow lawmakers rejected the proposal because it supposedly promotes principles of socialism. Policymakers must pass legislation to provide financial relief to Americans who are drowning in student debt, and citizens must make their elected officials more aware of their plight.

Safe Environments

Whether in a kindergarten class or a laboratory in college, all students perform better in safe environments that are conducive to teaching and learning. In the words of Dr. Ronald L. Epps, a retired educator, "There is nothing more egregious in education than for a child to lose life or limb." Thus, it is incumbent upon institutions of higher education to have processes and procedures in place to ensure the safety of all students.

One area that elicits serious concerns involves guns. In 2016, legislation was introduced in many states forcing colleges and universities to allow individuals with concealed-carry permits to bring their guns on campus. This will continue to be a contentious policy in higher education in upcoming years. While states like Tennessee and Ohio have approved some restrictions related to their campus weapons policies, legislation related to guns on campus failed in 14 others. However, pro-gun organizations have vowed to work to overturn these campus gun laws.

The stark reality is that carrying a concealed handgun in public—not on campuses—is permitted in all 50 states. Some states require gun owners to obtain permits while others have unrestricted carry and do not require permits. Proponents of conceal carry argue that criminals are less likely to attack someone they believe is armed. Opponents of concealed carry, however, argue that increased gun ownership leads to more gun crimes and unintended gun injuries.

As of 2017, eight states permit guns on college campuses. While there are variations in the content of the states' bills, the clear majority of campus stakeholders, including the law enforcement community, do not support allowing guns on college campuses in any capacity. Frankly, I am against allowing concealed handguns on campuses. Most college students are young adults who are still searching for their individual identify. During this maturation process, conflicts with peers often emerge that can result in arguments. The chances of these arguments becoming lethal increase tremendously when handguns are present. Therefore, state policymakers and officials in higher education must make an unwavering commitment to enacting polices that keep our campuses safe and free of guns, sexual assaults, drugs, and all forms of physical violence.

Poverty

The all-too-familiar phrase "poor college student" has been part of higher education lexicon for many years. It conjures up images of the economic challenges college students face, such as surviving on a diet that includes ramen noodles and peanut butter sandwiches. Those economic challenges still exist because many college students today are extremely poor, and in many instances, may not have a place to sleep at night.

According to a recent census, about 15.2 percent of the total U.S. population has an income below the poverty level. Furthermore, over half (51.8 percent) of the students who were living independently off campus struggled below the poverty line. The poverty rate for counties with high proportions of college students is negatively impacted when off-campus students are factored into the statistics. For example, in Monroe County, Indiana, home of Indiana University, the poverty rate is 25.5 percent. However, it drops to 13.8 percent when the figures for off-campus college students are subtracted. Likewise, the poverty rate for Centre County, Pennsylvania, home of Penn State University, is 20.2 percent, but it plunges to 9.8 percent without off-campus college students.

The data provides a glimpse of the high poverty rate among college students. Hunger and homelessness are often byproducts of poverty. In 2016, four campus-based organizations conducted a comprehensive study examining the prevalence and impact of poverty among college students. It was one of the broadest research studies of this issue to date. The sample for the study included surveys taken from nearly 3,800 students who were attending 8 community colleges and 26 four-year institutions across 12 states.

According to the report, "Hunger on Campus", nearly half of the students surveyed were food insecure and 22 percent qualified as hungry, meaning they had the very lowest level of food security. Moreover, it was discovered that food insecurity or uncertainty even extended to students who were employed, participated in a campus meal plan, or sought other financial assistance. It was further reported that food insecurity was more prevalent among students of color. Fifty-seven percent of African American students reported food insecurity, as compared to 40 percent of white students.

Clearly, poverty, hunger, and homelessness are a reality for far too many American college students. Undoubtedly, these factors have the potential of wreaking havoc on the success of hundreds of thousands of students in higher education. While many colleges have food banks and pantries for needy students, governmental entities must do more to support the thousands of college students who need assistance with basic living essentials. It's an opportunity for higher education officials and lawmakers to explore solutions to help the most economically vulnerable students on our college campuses.

Several colleges have developed some innovative programs to address the food uncertainty or insecurity that exists for many students. For example, Oregon State University and Humboldt State University (California) have on-campus stores that accept food stamps. At California State University in Fresno, students have access to a mobile app that will notify them when an on-campus catered event ends, and there is leftover food available. At this point, as a nation, we should accept the fact that many college students are in a crisis and need help with basic living. It is now incumbent upon lawmakers and officials in higher education to develop strategies and enact legislation to help college students meet those basic living needs of food and shelter.

Personnel and Instruction

In his 1977 book titled *Why the Professor Can't Teach*, Morris Kline blamed "the overemphasis on research" as the primary reason for the poor quality of undergraduate education in America. He was especially critical of tenured professors for ignoring their obligations to students by teaching courses in a way that reflected their own interests and biases. Not much has changed 40 years later.

The fact remains that college professors continue to operate under the "publish or perish" paradigm; that is, publish articles in journals or your employment at the college will perish. They are being paid to publish, not to teach. Most professors consider teaching a disruption to their research, which is what's most important to them. Even at liberal arts and community colleges where teaching is supposed to be the most important thing professors do, administrators pressure faculty to publish.

It is fairly safe to say that most high school graduates choose their institutions of higher education based on the availability of their preferred major, the ability to get a good job, and whether the faculty are good teachers or mentors. These student-applicants are not really concerned about the number of books or articles the professors have published. Besides, no evidence suggests that professors who are conducting research are better undergraduate teachers because of it.

If teaching matters, then much-needed changes must occur in college classrooms. Frankly, most professors have not been taught the principles of teaching adult learners. In many instances, undergraduate classes are taught by graduate students and new college professors who simply are not prepared to teach. For most institutions, the primary expectation for their faculty is to have PhDs, which only amplifies a major flaw in current higher education. A PhD is a research degree whose recipients are highly trained specialists. Contrary to the myth that persists, holders of this degree are not expert teachers. In most cases, they are adequate teachers at best.

Frankly, I'm not sure what the requirements are for becoming a college professor today. Whatever they are, I don't think the requirements are as stringent today as in previous years. More than ever, colleges operate under a business model. As businesses, they want to make money by enrolling as many students as possible. The more students they enroll, the more revenue they receive through tuition, endowments, and supplementary fees. Because it would be difficult to pack 750 students into one freshman history course, many colleges today try to adjust by hiring as many adjunct "professors" as possible to teach lower-level classes.

Therefore, many college departments today are staffed with a substantial number of part-time instructors with limited teaching experience. To make matters worse, many colleges simply select graduate students and shove them into undergraduate teaching positions. This is truly a form of "the blind leading the blind." In this scenario, college students are paying full tuition to be taught by other college students.

In many instances, college students could receive superior instruction in lower-level classes taught by experienced high school teachers as opposed to being taught by inexperienced graduate students. This provides a compelling argument for dual enrollment courses. Such courses provide opportunities for high school students to take college-level courses and earn concurrent credit toward a high school diploma and a college degree.

Dual enrollment courses are primarily available to eligible eleventh- or twelfth-grade high school students. In some limited cases, ninth- and tenth-grade students are permitted to take the courses. They may enroll full-time or part-time in credit-bearing college-level courses that are approved by a state's board of education. These courses may be taken either before, during, or after regular school hours. These courses may also be taken on the college campus, online, or at the high school during the regular school calendar year.

Dual enrollment courses can potentially address three issues that currently haunt many institutions of higher education. First, the courses will address issues related to college affordability. These dual enrollment courses are free and enable students to start accumulating college credits while in high school. Second, experienced teachers, not graduate students, teach the courses. Third, students receive much-needed preparation for college. Not only do they receive quality instruction, they get an idea of what full-time college coursework will be like.

Chapter Summary and Action Needed

Undoubtedly, given the complexities involved with America's system of higher education, there is no quick fix to the many challenges that exist. However, there are several reforms that could be implemented to address some of the issues related to governance, student poverty, instruction, and curriculum.

The primary issue related to governance is college affordability. The vast majority of colleges are unaffordable for working class families. Lawmakers must develop legislation and policies that would make higher education more of a right for all citizens as opposed to a luxury for a privileged few. One of the surest ways to boost college affordability is to make certain that students complete their degrees as quickly as possible.

Today, the country spends an enormous amount of money educating students who ultimately drop out before graduation. Only 60 percent of American undergraduates seeking a bachelor's degree complete their studies within six years, and 30 percent of students seeking an associate's degree finish within three years.

Poverty is also an issue that has wreaked havoc on many students, both during and after their time in college. While in college, many students experience major challenges related to basic living needs such as food and shelter. Hunger and homelessness are harsh realities for far too many college students. Lawmakers and officials in higher education must leave their state of denial and accept the fact that many students are in crisis and need help. Much-needed help can come in the form of legislation, policies, and opportunities that would enable needy students greater access to food and shelter. In America, it is inexcusable that our future leaders must endure such hardships—even convicted criminals have free shelter and three meals per day!

The after-school poverty for many college students manifests in the form of loan debts. An entire generation is being crippled by their student loan debts. In 2016, the total U.S. student debt rose to a record-breaking $1.31 trillion, which marked the eighteenth year in a row it has risen. On average, more than two-thirds of the students leave college owing roughly $37,172. This debt seriously hampers their American Dream of achieving success and prosperity.

The final area in higher education that needs reform is curriculum and instruction. Too often, college students take courses for the sole purposes of earning credits, and those courses are often taught by professors who tend to focus more on conducting publication research rather than on teaching. Students typically receive grades based on their classroom attendance and ability to use rote memory to pass exams. The curriculum is less-than-rigorous, and the instruction often involves students "sitting-and-getting" information from a professor's lecture. Clearly, this antiquated model that exists in many institutions of higher education needs a facelift.

The operational model for America's system of higher education has remained virtually unchanged for nearly a century. Many institutions have become "diploma factories" that award degrees to students based on the number of hours spent in the classroom or online, not for their competency. State lawmakers and officials in higher education should consider following the lead of Wisconsin and move their colleges and universities to a competency-based degree model.

In this model, degrees are awarded based on competency in a particular subject area. Not only would this change the thinking in higher education, it would expedite degree completion and save money for students and taxpayers. Moreover, it would force college professors to leave the comforts of their research labs to engage their students in meaningful and relevant instruction. It would be worthwhile for governors, lawmakers, and educators to form a think tank to discuss the merits of moving toward a competency-based model for higher education in America.

CHAPTER 8

K–12 Public Education— Reform Actions Needed

While the rest of the developed world has continued to improve their schools and student learning, America's K–12 public education system has undergone little change since the 1970s. At one time, the United States was recognized as having a world-class system of public education. Our schools now rank 20th (out of 30 countries) in high school graduation rates, 24th in college graduation rates, and 27th in college graduation rates for scientists and engineers. The American model of the 180-day school year, the 1 teacher per 25 students (on average) ratio, the 6-hour school day with the same general subjects, and the same graduation requirements has resulted in our educational system becoming more obsolete. Obviously, meaningful reform is needed.

Any efforts to reform K–12 public education in America must consider the changing demographics of our country. In the 1970s, many public schools in America were wrestling with issues related to desegregation, and the student population was predominantly white. In 2014, the demographics reached a milestone when, for the first time, the majority of students in K–12 public education were nonwhite. This diversity wave has created a dynamic in public education that cannot be ignored—it is called multiculturalism. Cultural and racial diversity, along with poverty, are factors that must be addressed in any reform effort if America harbors any hopes of ever reclaiming its status as a world-class K–12 public education system.

The framework for discussing the reforms that are needed in K–12 public education must be conducted within the framework of four constructs— *policy and governance, poverty, personnel,* and *pedagogy*. Each factor will be discussed in a separate subsection of this chapter.

Policy and Governance

One issue that is gripping K–12 public education in America is the rash of out-of-school suspensions. National concern was triggered from data showing that blacks and Hispanics are far more likely to be suspended and expelled from school. As a direct result of these out-of-school suspensions, black and Hispanic students are far more likely to drop out of high school. In addition, schools have begun to employ more police officers to enforce their "zero tolerance" student discipline codes. It has resulted in more students being arrested and criminal charges filed against them. This connection between police or school resource officers (SROs) has been dubbed the *school-to-prison pipeline*.

If school districts truly want to reform discriminatory practices related to these disproportionate suspensions and arrests of children of color, they must do so through their policies and procedures. Whether elected or appointed, the primary responsibility of any school board is governance. As such, the school board's charge is to develop policies that are designed to ensure that all students, regardless of their race, creed, color, religion, socioeconomic status, or gender, have equal access to a quality K–12 public education. It, then, becomes the superintendent's responsibility to develop procedures ensuring that all schools implement the board's policies without bias, prejudice, or discrimination.

School boards speak through their policies, and their words should become the rule for all employees. Any form of noncompliance should be grounds for employee termination, including the superintendent. Members of school boards should be advocates for all children, and their policies should reflect an intolerance for any form of disparate treatment of any child. Unfortunately, many public education systems have attempted to shape the climate in their schools through rigid law and order policies with threats of harsh punishment. These zero-tolerance policies typically create more problems than they solve.

Zero-tolerance policies were developed in the 1990s in response to school shootings and general fears about crime. In 1994, the federal government passed the Gun Free Schools Act, which requires schools to expel any student who brought a gun to campus. During that time, the "broken windows" theory of law enforcement became popular. The idea was that cracking down on minor violations prevented serious crimes. Hence, school systems began to rewrite their policies enabling administrators to impose harsh consequences (i.e., long-term suspension or expulsion) for minor misbehaviors.

While zero-tolerance policies were intended to make schools safer places for teaching and learning, researchers have not found any conclusive evidence to support that desired outcome. In fact, as an unintended consequence, suspension rates have actually increased during the twenty-first century. According the U. S. Department of Education, roughly 20 percent of all students in grades 6 through 12 will be suspended in any given school year. A massive study in Texas showed that over half (54 percent) of that state's students were suspended or expelled at least once during middle and high school. Very few of the infractions or violations of school rules involved weapons, and most involved behaviors that previously resulted in some sort of a verbal reprimand.

Increasingly, educators have begun to conclude that zero tolerance does not work. Many school systems across the nation have begun to institute more flexible practices like "restorative justice", which focus on repairing harm, restoring relationships, and helping students become accountable for their actions. In 2015, the Dallas (TX) Independent School District used restorative discipline programs to address discipline in six of their elementary and middle schools. The results speak for themselves:

- In-school suspensions dropped by 70 percent
- Out-of-school suspensions dropped by 77 percent
- The number of students sent to alternative schools decreased by 50 percent

Clearly, policies can make a difference. If school boards truly want to govern and make the health, safety, and welfare of children their top priority, they can do so through their policies. Comprehensive student-focused policies can (a) condemn the disparate treatment of children of color, (b) close the school-to-prison pipeline, (c) reduce the number of suspensions and student arrests, (d) keep students in school and engaged in classroom instruction, and (e) foster the development of processes to improve graduation rates. All of this can be done through leadership, governance, and policies.

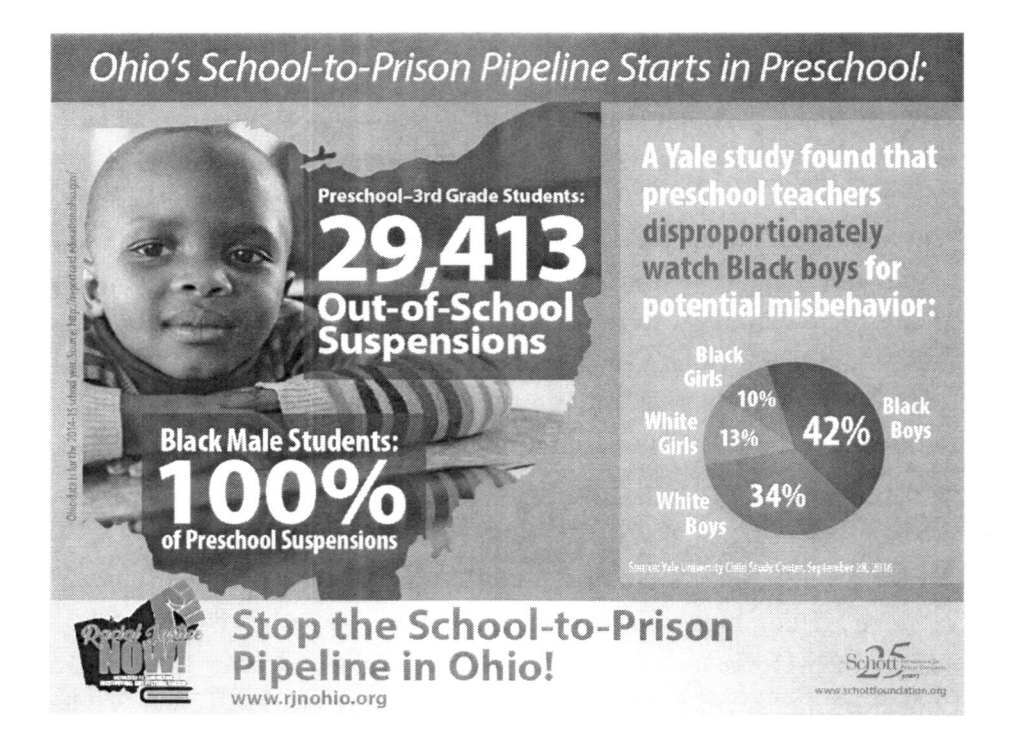

Ohio's School-to-Prison Pipeline Starts in Preschool:

Preschool–3rd Grade Students: **29,413** Out-of-School Suspensions

Black Male Students: **100%** of Preschool Suspensions

A Yale study found that preschool teachers disproportionately watch Black boys for potential misbehavior:

- Black Girls: 10%
- White Girls: 13%
- Black Boys: 42%
- White Boys: 34%

Source: Yale University Child Study Center, September 28, 2016

Stop the School-to-Prison Pipeline in Ohio!
www.rjnohio.org

The reform process should not be difficult because all school boards can write a comprehensive non–zero tolerance policy for student discipline that could address arrests and the disparate treatment of any subgroup of students. The board policy should be clear, concise, and uniformly enforced. The policy for a school district's Student Discipline Code should include a policy statement, statement indicating the scope of the code, list of rules infractions that warrant a disciplinary consequence, and a process for requesting an appeal of a suspension or expulsion.

Policy Statement

As previously stated, a school board speaks through its policy. The discipline code must contain a definitive statement indicating the board's expectations for the nondiscriminatory enforcement of its policy. The statement should be similar to the following:

> The School Board is committed to creating a safe, positive environment for all students, staff, parents, stakeholders, and community partners. The Board complies with all federal and state laws, and provides an equal opportunity for all students. The Board prohibits any form of discrimination in admission; grading; discipline; and any other activity based on race, creed, color, national origin, religion, ancestry, age, marital status, sexual orientation (known or perceived), gender identity expression (known or perceived), gender, handicap, nationality, or citizenship. Finally, any employee who willfully violates this policy statement is subject to immediate termination.

Scope of the Code

The scope should stipulate when the Board's rules and regulations governing student discipline are effective. Typically rules and regulations are effective on school grounds at any time, at a school bus stop, on a school bus during a school activity, en route to and/or from school or a school activity, and off school grounds while a student is participating in or attending a school-sponsored or school-related event. In short, the discipline code should be enforced from door-to-door—from the time students leave the doors of their homes until the time they return to that same door after dismissal of school.

Rules

When there is a lack of structure, chaos and confusion follows. This is especially true when school discipline rules are vague and subject to personal interpretation. School rules should be well-defined and presented in such a way that everyone (i.e., students, teachers, parents, administrators, and stakeholders) is aware of the punishment that corresponds with any given rule violation. For example, each rule could be placed into one of the three following categories:

Rule Violation	**Minor**	**Moderate**	**Major**
Cutting class	X		
Bullying		X	
Possession of a gun			X

Each category—minor, moderate, and major—should have a corresponding school-board–approved range of punishment for each rule violation. For example, the punishment for violating a minor discipline rule, such as cutting class, could range from the student (regardless of race, gender, or religion) receiving a warning or as much as two days of in-school suspension. The punishment for being in possession of a gun would constitute a major rule violation, and the student (regardless of race, gender, or religion) must appear before a disciplinary hearing officer or tribunal to determine the most appropriate punishment.

Understandably, developmental differences must factor into student discipline codes. A first grader bullying another first grader is different from a seventh grader bullying another seventh grader. School systems should consider having a separate discipline code for elementary, middle, and high schools. Each code should have well-defined rules with a corresponding range of consequences or punishment for violations. Most importantly, the school board must mandate that all forms of discipline be issued without any discrimination related to the student's race, religion, color, gender, or socioeconomic status.

Appeals Process

In our democratic society, a student never loses the right to basic fairness. In *Goss v Lopez (1975)*, the U.S. Supreme Court ruled that a due process hearing is required for any student facing long suspension or exclusion (i.e., 10 days or more). This federal law must be included in any student discipline code. A student should also have the right to appeal any suspension of three days or more to the principal or a district-level staff member. Finally, the student must have the opportunity to file an appeal to the local school board for any suspension of 10 days or more.

Police Involvement

The principal, not the school resource officer, should set the tone for creating the school's environment for teaching and learning. School discipline should be handled by school staff. The state of Georgia recognized this when legislators updated its Juvenile Justice Reform Bill in 2014. As part of the reform, the bill stipulated that school resource officers were prohibited from getting involved with a school discipline issue unless it involved a criminal act such as a sexual assault or distribution of a controlled substance.

In their policies, school boards should ensure there is a clear distinction between the role of an administrator and an SRO. An administrator should handle violations of the Student Discipline Code, and SROs should only handle situations in which an alleged criminal act was reported. This simple policy could dramatically decrease the number of student arrests in public schools and virtually dismantle the school-to-prison pipeline.

Action Needed: The importance of a school board's policy cannot be overstated. School boards across America must understand that their primary responsibility is to serve as advocates for all children, regardless of their race, religion, color, gender, or socioeconomic status. To that end, their policies for student discipline must be written and enforced in a manner that guarantees the fair and nondiscriminatory treatment of all children.

Poverty

Fifty-two years after President Johnson declared a war on poverty, American children continue to struggle with issues that are either directly or indirectly related to poverty. In fact …

- The child poverty today is only 5 percent less than in 1964.
- The U.S. infant mortality rate is still one of the highest among industrialized nations.
- The U.S. teen birth rate is still among the highest in industrialized nations.
- The percent of children living in single-parent households has more than doubled.
- The majority of fourth and eighth graders from poor families continue to read below grade level.
- Black children remain three times more likely than white children to be poor.

Poverty is a complicated issue that continues to have a debilitating effect on children, especially in areas related to school achievement. Research findings indicate that children who are raised in poverty are at an increased risk of a wide range of outcomes that are identified at birth and can extend into adulthood. It is imperative for educators to become familiar with the poverty-related factors that negatively impact student achievement. More importantly, school districts should make provisions in their policies, practices, and procedures to address four negative outcomes that are associated with poverty, which include 1) school readiness, 2) academic achievement, 3) dropouts, and 4) graduation from high school.

School Readiness

Research indicates that poor children are more likely than their more affluent peers to be raised by parents who have completed fewer years of education and grow up in households that are less cognitively stimulating. As early as 24 months, children in low-income families have been found to show lags in their cognitive development when compared to their peers. By age three, a child from a low-income household has heard 30 million fewer words than his or her higher-income peers. This is significant because the brain's most critical stage of development is in early childhood. By age five, roughly 48 percent of poor children are ready for school as compared to 75 percent of children from families with moderate and high income.

If poor children are at a distinct disadvantage in their readiness for school, it would seem practical for districts to offer early intervention programs. There is a growing body of research that indicates investing in high-quality pre-kindergarten (pre-K) education yields positive benefits for children, schools, and communities. According to reports compiled by the Center for Public Education, children who participate in high-quality pre-K programs enter school more prepared to learn than their peers. More specifically, studies have shown that children who attended a pre-K program scored higher on reading and math tests than children who merely received parental care.

Research further indicates that the positive effects of early childhood programs are far-reaching and long-term. In a classic longitudinal study in North Carolina in the 1970s known as the Abecedarian Project, a sample of children from disadvantaged homes were placed in a high-quality preschool program from infancy to age five. After completing the early intervention program, the researchers tracked the children's development at intervals up to age 35. The findings indicated that when compared to children who did not participate in the preschool program, the Abecedarian kids were less likely to have repeated a grade, need special education, or gotten into trouble with the law. These results speak volumes for the need for schools to provide early enrichment to their students before they enter kindergarten. The programs are a long-term investment in the future of children who come from disadvantage circumstances.

Action Needed: It is imperative for school systems to offer early enrichment and early learning opportunities to better prepare children for kindergarten. Lawmakers and education officials must ensure that all children in high-poverty areas have access to a public school-operated Pre-Kindergarten or Early Childhood Education program.

Academic Achievement

The relationship between poverty and academic achievement is well-chronicled. Historically, as a group, low-income students have not performed as well as high-income students on most measures of academic success such as standardized test scores, grades, and college completion rates. In most school districts, students from low-income families attend Title I schools. Students in these schools tend to perform lower than their peers in non-Title I schools on most measures of academic achievement.

Action Needed: Title I schools need more instructional resources and more highly qualified teachers who are trained in instructional strategies necessary to engage the culturally and linguistically diverse students in schools with high-poverty populations.

Graduation from High School

According to a report from Grad-Nation, the Class of 2012 marked the first time ever that the graduation rate in America's public schools reached 80 percent. While that's good news, there is one glaring caveat, and it involves poverty. Table 12 lists the "adjusted cohort" graduation rates for poor vs. non-poor students in selected states. In most states, a double-digit gap existed between low-income students and others. The average gap between poor and nonpoor students was 15.6 percentage points. Ohio,

Minnesota, and Colorado had the largest gaps. Overall, 45 states had double-digit graduation gaps between low-income and other students.

Not surprisingly, research indicates that school absences have a more debilitating effect on children in poverty when compared to their more affluent peers. Children who miss 10 percent of kindergarten tend to perform poorly through fifth grade. By middle and high school, absences become a key predictor of who will drop out of school. In addition, children between the ages of 16 and 18 who come from low-income families are seven times more likely to drop out of school than those from high-income families. Compelling evidence found in the research literature indicates that poverty and student absences work in tandem to stifle the graduation rates for children who come from low-income families.

Table 12

Adjusted Cohort Graduation Rates (Percentages) for the Class of 2012

State	Low Income Students	Other Students	Gap
Alabama	66	85	-19
Arkansas	79	89	-10
California	73	86	-13
Colorado	61	85	-24
Florida	65	82	-17
Georgia	61	79	-18
Illinois	73	88	-15
Louisiana	66	78	-12
Maryland	75	88	-13
Minnesota	59	87	-28
Mississippi	70	81	-11
New Jersey	75	88	-13
New York	68	84	-16
North Carolina	75	84	-9
Ohio	68	89	-21
Pennsylvania	74	89	-15
South Carolina	68	82	-14
Tennessee	82	94	-12
Texas	85	91	-6
Virginia	77	88	-11

Note. The adjustment involved converting the leaver rate (5 years) to the cohort rate (4 years)

Fortunately, there are resources available to improve the graduation rates for poor students. The National Dropout Prevention Center/Network at Clemson University provides many evidence-based strategies and resources that school systems can use to address issues related to dropout prevention. On its website, the center lists the following "15 effective strategies" for dropout prevention:

- A Systemic Approach
- School-Community Collaboration
- Safe Learning Environments
- Family Engagement
- Early Literacy Development
- Early Childhood Education
- Mentoring/Tutoring
- Service Learning
- Alternative Schooling
- Afterschool/Out-of-School Opportunities
- Professional Development
- Active Learning
- Educational Technology
- Individualized Instruction
- Career and Technical Education

While organizations like the National Dropout Prevention Center/Network offer strategies to prevent dropouts, there are agencies that also recover students who have dropped out and offer them the opportunity to earn their high school diploma. One noteworthy agency that provides both dropout prevention and recovery services to school districts is Catapult Learning, Inc. In its dropout recovery program, this agency will go into the community and actively encourage dropouts to resume pursuit of their diploma in their neighborhood school or in an academy Catapult operates. In this win-win situation, former dropouts earn a high school diploma, and the school district's graduation rate increases.

Action Needed: School districts must declare a state of emergency related to the graduation gap between their at-risk (i.e., impoverished) and more affluent students. Early intervention programs must be implemented to improve the academic development of students who are at-risk of dropping out. Post-intervention programs such as the one offered by Catapult Learning, Inc., and others should be explored to reconnect dropouts with public education.

Personnel and Pedagogy

Virtually everyone agrees that America's system of public education faces many challenges that have intensified since the beginning of the twenty-first century. Issues ranging from student discipline to budget cuts have created angst in school districts across the nation, and officials are trying to develop strategies to improve teaching and learning. Throughout this book, I have emphasized the importance of having competent teachers in classrooms because this is where the real work in K–12 public education occurs. Three factors must be addressed to improve teaching and learning in public education today: 1) the increasing culture gap between students and teachers, 2) the need for effective teacher training, and 3) an increasing lack of respect for the profession.

Culture Gap

In 2016, there were approximately 3.2 million public school teachers in the United States, which is slightly less than the 3.4 million in 2008 when the country was in the middle of a great recession. Racial disparities have also persisted in the teaching profession. In 2012, 83 percent of the teachers in America were white, and that figure dipped slightly to 82 percent in 2016. During that time, the percentage of Hispanic teachers increased the most to around 7 percent, while the percentage of black teachers continued to hover around 6 percent.

As previously stated, 2014 marked the first-time white students did not represent a majority in the nation's public schools. It also marked a time when greater attention was directed at the wide racial or culture gap between teachers and their students. (See Table 13.) In addition to racial disparities, teaching is still a predominantly female profession. In 2016, 76 percent of the teachers in public education were women, a slight increase from 74 percent in 2014. These racial and gender disparities have continually existed throughout the twenty-first century.

A recent conversation with my granddaughter, a tenth-grader, provides an African American student's perspective of the culture gap that exists in many schools in America today. Janai said, "Granddaddy, a lot of (white) teachers in my school think they know us, but they really don't. They try to talk like black people, but it's soooo embarrassing. It insults me because they must think all of us talk like rappers from Hip Hop Nation. It's just ridiculous."

While the actions of many teachers at Janai's school meant well, their lack of culture competence has inhibited their ability to bridge the culture gap between them and their students. While the profile for teachers in public education has remained white, middle-class, and monolingual English-speakers, the profile for students has become increasingly more ethnically and culturally diverse. In the absence of proper training, many teachers try to bridge the culture gap with an embrace of color-blindness or the Golden Rule—treating others the way they would want to be treated.

Culture really matters, and it is not just a list of holidays, religious traditions, or knowledge of urban language. It is a lived experience unique to everyone. A teacher's job is to stimulate the intellectual development of all children, which encompasses more than simply operating from a perspective of being color-blind. To truly engage students in the learning process, teachers must reach out to them in ways that are culturally and linguistically responsive and appropriate, and they must examine the cultural assumptions and stereotypes they take with them into the classroom.

Table 13

The Teacher-Student Racial Gap

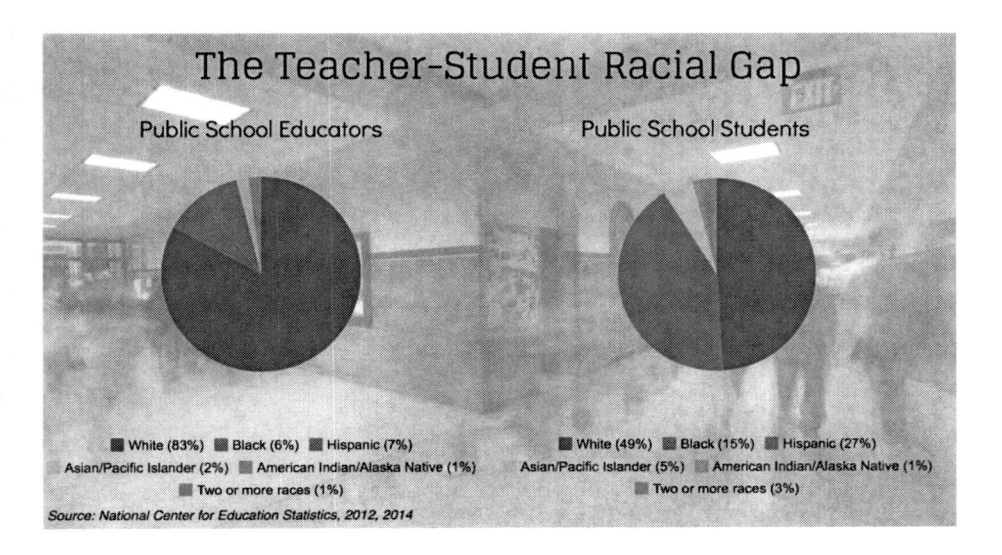

The Teacher-Student Racial Gap

Public School Educators
- White (83%)
- Black (6%)
- Hispanic (7%)
- Asian/Pacific Islander (2%)
- American Indian/Alaska Native (1%)
- Two or more races (1%)

Public School Students
- White (49%)
- Black (15%)
- Hispanic (27%)
- Asian/Pacific Islander (5%)
- American Indian/Alaska Native (1%)
- Two or more races (3%)

Source: National Center for Education Statistics, 2012, 2014

When students see their teachers as an ally in their quest for an education, they perform better. An excellent way to create this framework and bridge the culture gap between teachers and their students is through culturally responsive teaching (CRT). CRT is a thoughtful and deliberate approach that recognizes the individual needs of students. The National Center for Culturally Responsive Educational Systems provides the following description of CRT:

> Culturally responsive pedagogy and practice facilitates and supports the achievement of all students. In culturally responsive classrooms and schools, effective teaching and learning occur in a culturally supported, learner-centered context, whereby the strengths students bring to school are identified, nurtured, and utilized to promote student achievement.

The essence of CRT is to empower students educationally and to expand their skills in other domains such as the social and political awareness. Teachers accomplish this by making their students' own skills, languages, and attitudes meaningful in classroom instruction. Through this approach, teachers get to know students in a way that is personal and individual. Acknowledging and embracing a student's racial or ethnic background is important, but it is just a piece of who they are. Fully recognizing and respecting them means learning how they learn and what they are passionate about or interested in.

On December 10, 2015, President Obama signed the bipartisan Every Student Succeeds Act (ESSA) into law, which went into effect at the beginning of the current (2017-2018) school year. This new law gives new flexibility to states, which represents a big change from the No Child Left Behind Act. Under the new law, states, districts, and schools are required to monitor and report the academic performance of historically underserved groups of students based on their racial/ethnic status, socioeconomic status, English-language ability, and disability status. These requirements are aligned with the tenets of a culturally responsive pedagogy, which is focused on student achievement, affirmation of cultural identity, and development of critical perspectives. Without addressing these key tenets, it is highly unlikely that public schools are going to make a difference in the lives of historically underserved groups of students.

Action Needed: School districts should recognize the fact that student engagement is the key to learning in the classroom. The culture gap between teachers and their students impedes teaching and learning. Regardless of the level of diversity in the student population, school districts should offer and mandate that all teachers receive ongoing professional development in the principles of culturally responsive and culturally relevant pedagogy to help bridge the culture gap between them and their students.

Teacher Training Programs

During the past decade, teaching in public education has become more complex than at any point in our nation's history. Demands are higher than ever for teachers to be masters of often increasingly complicated content areas, as well as experts in emerging pedagogies and technologies such as blended and project-based learning. Moreover, teachers are expected to know how to teach all students from a wide range of cultural, social, linguistic, ethnic, and socioeconomic backgrounds. It is simply not realistic to expect any teacher to become proficient in these various areas without comprehensive training or ongoing professional development.

Given the challenges that teachers face in K–12 public education today, their preparation must involve two critically important components: 1) *knowledge of the subject* to be taught, and 2) knowledge and skill in *how to teach* that subject. Effective teachers understand and apply strategies to help increase student achievement. They understand and apply the principles of positive reinforcement to motivate and engage students. Additionally, effective teachers know how to diagnose their student's individual learning needs as well as create a stimulating learning environment.

This raises an age-old question with "nature-nurture" implications: Are effective classroom teachers born or made? The answer leans more toward the "made" axis of the dichotomy. Effective teachers are shaped through meaningful preservice and in-service training programs. They gain the bulk of the *knowledge of the subject* they teach through a preservice program, which is the supervised training a teacher receives while in college. Effective teachers refine their skills on *how to teach* through in-service programs, which is the ongoing training they receive while employed as a teacher.

Regardless of a teacher's performance in preservice or in-service programs, they must meet their state's requirements for certification or licensure. While specific requirements vary, each state's Board of Education typically requires prospective teachers to have at least a bachelor's degree, pass a background check, and earn a passing score on a state-approved teacher competency or licensing exam. The State of Georgia has a four-tier certification process that encourages teachers to improve their knowledge and skills. The four levels of certification are:

- *Preservice* (candidates must earn a bachelor's degree and complete a teacher preparation program)
- *Induction* (candidates must pass the state's written licensing exam)
- *Professional* (candidates must complete at least three years of successful teaching)
- *Advanced/Lead Profession* (candidates must have five years of teaching experience, an advanced degree, and earned a National Board for Professional Teaching Standards certification)

Due to a recent shortage of teachers in public education, educators and lawmakers are struggling with finding ways to attract and retain good teachers for low-performing schools. For various and sundry reasons, experienced teachers shy away from low-performing schools. Moreover, when inexperienced teachers are placed in a low-performing school, they seldom return after one year of employment. This is especially true when the inexperienced teacher is a white female who is assigned to a low-performing secondary school in a large urban district.

Although nearly every state has reported teacher shortages to the U.S. Department of Education, the problem is much more pronounced in some states than in others. Regardless of the state, students in high-poverty and high-minority schools are still hit hardest when there are teacher shortages. In 2014, less than 1 percent of teachers in low-minority schools on average were certified, while four times as many in high-minority schools were uncertified. Teacher attrition—the number of teachers leaving the profession for a variety of reasons—has remained high in 2017 and has been deemed the primary cause of the shortage.

Due to the shortage of teachers and the reluctance of experienced ones to teach in low-performing facilities, educators have explored alternative pathways to recruit and staff their schools. Several alternative pathways have emerged over the years to help people become teachers even if they did not start out on that path. Those alternative pathways include volunteers working with groups like Teach for America and programs for retired military personnel, as well as location-specific programs like the Academy for Urban School Leadership in Chicago.

In 2015, President Obama launched an initiative called the "Excellent Educators for All" that required all states to have quality teachers in the classrooms filled with poor and minority kids. Essentially, this initiative forced states to examine why poor and minority students received more inexperienced teachers, and it required them to develop strategies to fix the problem. Many states focused on reforming teacher preparation (preservice and in-service) as the first key step to improving quality. Here are five reforms that various states proposed:

1. *Determine the success of training programs.* The Indiana Department of Education proposed to survey new teachers and the principals who supervised them to evaluate the effectiveness of their state's teacher training program. Similarly, Massachusetts proposed to identify teachers who completed training programs and publish their students' achievement data in a public report.

2. *Create a "Grow Your Own" system.* Arkansas, Indiana, and Oklahoma proposed expanding programs to recruit high-performing high school students to enter the teaching profession. Some states placed a special focus on recruiting minority students to increase diversity in their teacher workforce.

3. *Improve faculty knowledge at teacher prep programs.* Kentucky announced it would have regional coaches work in partnership with teacher prep programs to teach faculty members about new standards and teacher evaluation systems.

4. *Make teacher candidates perform before they enter a classroom.* In its proposal, Missouri indicated that it would create a performance assessment to ensure aspiring teachers have the skills needed to provide quality classroom instruction.

5. *Change teacher prep courses and student teaching.* Maine's plan included assembling the state's education officials so they could evaluate the curriculum for the teacher preparation and ensure that new teachers have student-teaching experience in high-poverty school settings.

Several issues are entangled with teacher training programs or initiatives. First, attrition has created a national shortage of qualified teachers. Second, many teachers are having difficulty keeping up with ever-emerging and complicated pedagogies. Third, districts across the nation are struggling with trying to find teachers for hard-to-staff schools in highly diverse, low-income, and/or urban communities.

> "The secret in education lies in respecting the student."
> —Ralph Waldo Emerson

In America, we spend a great deal of time, money, and resources trying to seek ways to improve the quality of teaching and learning in our schools. During that process, unproven innovations, such as open-space classrooms in the 1970s and ability grouping in the 1990s, were employed to improve student outcomes. These innovations or "experiments" yielded underwhelming results, and for the most part, were discarded as educational fads. The only consistent factor educators have identified to positively impact student achievement is the role of the teacher. Their skill set, knowledge, and enthusiasm are critical in determining the success of the children they teach.

In the purest sense, teaching is all about engagement, getting children to listen, and turning on a student's "switch" to learning. The best investment any state or local school board can make is to get the most effective and talented teachers they can in front of all children, regardless of their ethnicity or socioeconomic status. Recruiting and retaining the best teachers must involve a two-pronged process.

The first prong involves preservice, which is the process of providing prospective teachers with meaningful college coursework and a diverse student-teaching experience. The second prong involves in-service, which is the process of providing ongoing professional development for teachers to hone their instructional skills and keep them abreast of best practices in the field of education. Good teachers are competent professionals who realize that they cannot pick-and-choose their students. My two daughters (Nikki and Brittany) are competent elementary school teachers who have adopted what they call a "skittles" approach to pedagogy. They want all "flavors" of students in their classroom because they embrace diversity.

Action Needed: States must avoid partisan politics and review their plans for "Excellent Education for All" to ensure that all minority and low-income kids have a quality teacher in front of them. School districts must do four things to ensure that all students have quality teachers: 1) Hire quality teachers from institutions with reputable preservice training programs; 2) recruit and assist a diverse group of applicants to pursue an alternative path to obtain teacher certification; 3) staff schools based on students' needs, not a teacher's preference; and 4) provide ongoing and comprehensive in-service training in best practices and the principles of multicultural education to all teachers.

Lack of Respect for the Teaching Profession

As I reflect on my childhood during the segregated era of the 1960s, I can recall how teachers were among the most highly respected professionals in African American communities, at least in Columbia, South Carolina. Everyone in my working-class neighborhood admired Mr. and Mrs. Bolden. Mr. Bolden was a teacher and the head football coach at the local high school, and Mrs. Bolden was the school's librarian. As educators, they were held in highest regard in the community. All parents, including mine, challenged their children to be studious like the Bolden's son, Charles Jr, who proved to be a great role model. He was the quarterback of his high school football team, a graduate from the U.S. Naval Academy where he earned the rank of major general, and later an astronaut with NASA.

Things have changed dramatically since my days as a student in public education. Teachers are not as revered as in years past, and many leave the profession to pursue other interests. According to the Pew Research Center, Americans have a declining interest in education. These conclusions are based on an analysis of data taken from the Program for International Student Assessment (PISA). PISA is a worldwide exam that is administered every three years to 15-year-olds in 72 countries to measure their achievement in reading, math, and science.

The results of the 2015 PISA testing indicate that American students continue to lag behind their counterparts in other industrialized countries in the world, especially in math and science. Many educators used these findings to support the view that our students' relatively low performance is due to their waning interest in education. Other nationally renowned educators such as Dr. Steven Paine have argued that money is not the answer to boosting our country's status on the international educational stage. In studying the world's highest achievers (i.e., Finland, Singapore, Hong Kong, Japan, and Canada), Paine concludes that "our lack of respect for teachers" is the number-one enemy of education in America.

In his report, he cited Finland as a country where teachers are highly respected and afforded a status comparable to what is given to doctors and lawyers. He further reported that the teaching profession in Singapore is highly competitive and selective, and all teachers must meet high standards for skills in knowledge and instruction. The study on Japan revealed similar findings. Paine concluded that countries with the highest PISA results have been most successful in promoting teaching an attractive profession.

While an analysis of PISA scores can provide some insight regarding America's status on the world's stage of education, more information is needed before we can draw conclusions regarding the perceived status of teachers in the United States. To do that, we would have to go directly to the source. In 2016, the nonprofit Center on Education Policy (CEP) went directly to the source when they conducted online interviews with a nationally representative sample of 3,328 public school teachers in the United States. Their report paints a bleak picture of the American teaching profession, indicating that many teachers perceive the profession as becoming more demanding and stressful.

According to this report, nearly half of the teachers indicated they would leave the profession as soon as possible if they could get a higher-paying job elsewhere. Many teachers believed that stress and disappointments involved in teaching at their school was not worth the pay they received. Most of the stress and disappointment was due to what they described as trying to hit a "target that is constantly moving." Nearly half of the teachers cited state and district policies that hindered—not helped—teaching as among their most significant challenges.

The concerns expressed by the teachers in the CEP report appear to be reaching student-teachers in many teacher preparation programs. A growing number of student-teachers decline opportunities to enter the profession after they complete their supervised internship. Many cite concerns with student discipline, excessive paperwork, and a lack of respect and support from administrators. In their words, "It's just not worth it." This has contributed to the current national shortage of teachers as well as having created holes in the pipeline to the teacher workforce.

Clear evidence indicates that a lack of respect (real or perceived) has caused prospective teachers to evade the profession and active teachers to leave it. These factors, in turn, have required states to explore ways to fill shortages. In a recent edition of *The Wall Street Journal* (September 6, 2017), it was reported that several states were relaxing their credential requirements to make it easier for people to become licensed to teach in public education. Those states include Arizona, Connecticut, Illinois, and Minnesota. Arguably, the acts of desperation by these states only provide a temporary solution to the problem. In many cases, children will receive less-than-quality instruction, and in the absence of substantive reforms, there is no guarantee that the "poorly certified" teachers will remain in the profession.

Teaching conditions have plunged in the United States in terms of salaries, working conditions, and respect for the profession—all of which would attract and retain a stronger and more sustainable teaching workforce. Salaries ranked eighth among the top nine reasons outgoing teachers cited as the source of job dissatisfaction. In a 2016 report compiled by the Center for Public Education, the top nine reasons outgoing teachers cited for job dissatisfaction included:

1. Dissatisfied with administration (66 percent)
2. Dissatisfied with accountability/testing (60.5 percent)
3. Lack of influence and autonomy (51.6 percent)
4. Classroom intrusions (50.1 percent)
5. Student discipline problems (48.2 percent)
6. Poor facilities and resources (47.2 percent)
7. Dissatisfied with teaching assignment (40.6 percent)
8. Poor salary/benefits (29.5 percent)
9. Class sizes are too large (29.4 percent)

How do teachers reclaim the viability and respect that existed when the Boldens taught in the 1960s? I can't think of any other profession where college-educated people are questioned, second-guessed, and blamed as much as teachers. Unlike the Boldens, teachers today are overworked, underpaid, and underappreciated. Most egregiously, they feel left out of policy decisions that directly affect them. This conjures up memories of a slogan that reverberated throughout America during the 1770s: "Taxation without representation is tyranny." For teachers in 2017, the slogan could be "Policies without representation is tyranny."

Although there are no instant solutions to this problem, a change in the mind-set regarding teachers must involve leadership at the state and local levels of educational oversight. State-level officials must do their part by making a "statement" expressing how they value and respect the teaching profession. They can make this statement by implementing a competitive teacher salary schedule to attract college students and others to the profession. In addition, local level officials (i.e., school boards) can make similar statements through policies to also show respect for the profession and reward high-performing teachers.

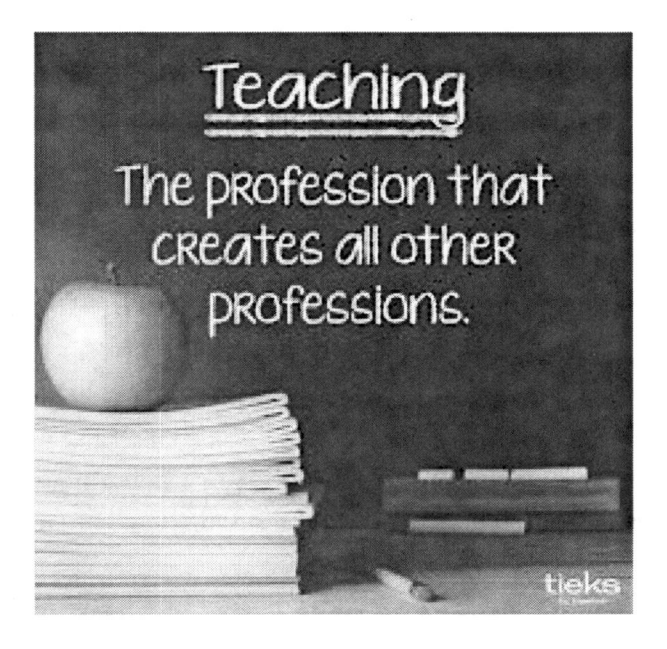

Teaching
The profession that creates all other professions.

While the reforms or "statements" at the state and local levels would serve to attract new teachers, it is equally as important (if not more) to retain the teachers that are already working in the public education system. Thus, leadership at school levels is an essential ingredient in any effort to rebuild the sense of pride and respect teachers formerly held for their profession. Effective principals set the tone in their schools that encourages respect, professional collaboration, and continuous improvement.

TNTP, formerly known as The New Teacher Project, compiled a list of eight low-cost proven strategies that administrators can use to retain teachers. They found that highly effective teachers who experienced two or more of the following strategies remained in their schools twice as long as those who did not:

- Provide regular, positive feedback to teachers.
- Help teachers identify areas of development.
- Give informal critical feedback about performance.
- Recognize accomplishments publicly.
- Inform teachers when they are highly effective.
- Provide leadership roles opportunities to teachers.
- Assign important responsibilities or opportunities to lead projects.
- Provide access to additional classroom resources.

In conclusion, teachers across America have begun to experience a sense of disenfranchisement and a lack of respect for the profession they have chosen. It has created a national shortage of teachers, both in schools and training programs that prepare them for the rigors of the profession. Today, there are challenges related to recruiting new teachers into the profession as well as retaining those that are currently teaching in K–12 classrooms. Until (and unless) the profession is placed on a higher plane and garners the respect it deserves, this shortage will continue, and many children will not receive a quality education.

Action Needed: Local and state officials must collaborate to make the teaching profession more attractive and respected. It can be done by making the profession more financially rewarding and less stressful. Regarding remuneration, state and local officials should review their salary schedules for teachers and adjust them to make the salaries for teaches more attractive and competitive. Also, stress levels can be reduced by training administrators to be more supportive, accommodating, and sensitive to the needs of teachers under their charge.

Chapter Summary

Although most students today probably have never used an encyclopedia, they were highly sought-after books in the twentieth century, which was sort of a golden age for their use as a vehicle to access educational information. During that time, such books became cheaper and people wanted them more. Encyclopedias were very popular because they provided an effective and compact way of conveying information. Today, however, the internet has made encyclopedias a mere figment of our past. Bookstores rarely sell these relics anymore, and charities even have a hard time giving them away.

In some ways, America's public education system has traveled a path similar to the one traveled by encyclopedias. Many of the practices in twentieth century, such as ability grouping and zero tolerance policies, have caused our educational system to remain stagnant. Instead of the internet, however, our educators' failure to adapt to the ever-increasing diversity (cultural and ethnic) has resulted in the continued use of ineffective and obsolete twentieth-century pedagogical practices. America's K–12 system of public education needs to be reformed with twenty-first century strategies.

The areas of reform that are needed in America's K–12 public education system can be placed into three major categories: policy and governance, poverty, and personnel and pedagogy. These major categories are, indeed, multifaceted. Therefore, some of the identified problems that need reform are rooted in more than one sub-category. For example, challenges related to diversity and teaching students from low-income families were manifested in the analysis of each of the three major categories. Reform solutions for each subcategory in the three major categories were provided in the form of action-needed statements.

The section on *policy and governance* focused on the "pink elephant" in the room of public education, which is the disparate treatment of children of color. Black and Hispanic children are far more likely to be suspended or expelled from school than their white counterparts. In addition, law enforcement officers are summoned more often when children of color violate a school rule. Their involvement increases the probability of an arrest that places the student in the infamous school-to-prison pipeline or juvenile justice system.

The national increase in out-of-school suspensions and expulsions is due in large part to discriminatory and ineffective zero tolerance policies that many school systems seem to favor. Since the primary responsibility of school boards is governance and advocacy for children, they have the authority to set policies with mandates prohibiting the disparate treatment of children, regardless of their race, religion, ethnicity, gender (known or perceived), socioeconomic status, or disability. The key components for writing and enforcing a comprehensive nondiscriminatory policy for student discipline were presented in this chapter.

In addition, the devastating impact of *poverty* in public education was also discussed. Like discipline, this complicated issue primarily strikes children of color, especially in areas related to school achievement. Children from low-income families tend to enter kindergarten at a low level of readiness. They are more at risk for having a pattern of low achievement in school, and ultimately, dropping out. Research findings indicate that children from low-income families are seven times more likely to drop out of school than those from more affluent families. Several best practices were presented to address dropout prevention and recovery.

There is no denying the fact that "teaching matters" in public education. The last section of this chapter, *personnel and pedagogy*, discussed challenges that exist and the twenty-first century reforms that are needed to improve teaching and learning for all children in K–12 public education. One of the greatest challenges in pedagogy or classroom instruction involves the culture gap between teachers and the students in their classrooms. Nationally, while nearly 83 percent of the teachers in public education are white, 51 percent of the students are nonwhite. This dynamic has created a problem in which many white teachers are having difficulty engaging their minority students in classroom instruction. Simply put, engaged students are learning, and those that are not engaged are not learning.

Increasing demands, which have been placed on teachers, have created a national shortage in the teaching profession. Teachers are avoiding and leaving the field of teaching for a variety of reasons, primarily due to a pervasive lack of respect (both real and perceived) that society has for the profession. Several strategies for reform were offered that state and local officials can implement to attract and retain good teachers. In the absence of meaningful and substantive reforms, America's system of K–12 public education will continue to erode, and our children will continue to lag behind their peers from many industrialized countries around the world.

CHAPTER 9

C. A. Johnson Preparatory Academy: Reviving an All-Black Urban High School

C. A. Johnson High School (CAJ) was established in 1949 as one of two high schools to serve black students in racially segregated Columbia, South Carolina. For various and sundry reasons, most of the city's more affluent black families attended CAJ. The first graduating class totaled 102 students. The school thrived during its first 30 years with an average enrollment that hovered around 1,100 students and was recognized throughout the state for its record of developing well-rounded black scholars, student-athletes, and entertainers. Some notable graduates with national prominence in their respective fields include NASA Astronaut General Charles F. Bolden, Entertainer J. Anthony Brown, Singer Angie Stone, and countless educators, lawyers, and commissioned officers in the military.

By the early 1980s, the school had undergone a noticeable transformation. Although every high school in Columbia was desegregated, CAJ remained a *de facto* racially segregated school. Most of the affluent blacks had moved into the suburbs and their children were enrolled in the predominantly white schools in their attendance zone. By the late 1990s, the enrollment at CAJ had plummeted, the state had repeatedly dubbed it a "failing" school, and the local school board entertained the notion of shutting it down.

In August 2000, the superintendent of Richland County (Columbia, SC) School District One recognized the need to reclaim the viability of CAJ, which was the last historically all-black high school that was active in South Carolina from the era of racial segregation. The superintendent gave me the task of reviving CAJ and transforming it into a mecca for teaching and learning. As a graduate of the CAJ Class of 1966,

I accepted the challenge with enthusiasm and became the seventh principal in the school's storied history.

With the support of many people, we were able to successfully turnaround my alma mater—a low-income, all-black, urban school—by creating a structure that was characterized by students assuming a voracious appetite for knowledge and teachers taking pride in their ability to deliver that knowledge. In this chapter, I outline the steps we used to reclaimed CAJ's viability, and I challenge other school leaders to follow my blueprint if they sincerely want to improve outcomes for their disadvantaged students whose hidden talents lie dormant and are ready to be activated.

The Charge

When Dr. Ronald L. Epps became the superintendent of Richland County School District One (Richland One) in 1999, he came by way of Rockford, Illinois, with a vision to make each of the 44 schools in the district a haven for teaching and learning. Dr. Epps had earned national recognition as a brilliant, no-nonsense leader. Shortly after his arrival, he expressed concerns that CAJ was one of the lowest-performing schools in the district. In addition, it also had a reputation for having severe problems related to student discipline and teacher apathy. Dr. Epps made it clear to me and other members of his cabinet that "when one school struggles; we all struggle."

Near the end of his first year as superintendent, Dr. Epps realized that some significant changes needed to occur at CAJ, otherwise, the school would sink further into its abyss. He summoned me to his office and asked me to lead a task force with the charge to create a "renaissance" for CAJ by forming a partnership with Benedict College, which is an HBCU located roughly three miles from the high school's campus. A seven-member task force was commissioned that consisted of three district-level administrators (deputy superintendent, area superintendent, and director of curriculum and instruction), the CAJ principal (Murray Smith), two professors from Benedict College (Drs. Jan Witty and Ronnie Hopkins), and me (Dr. Jim Taylor, assistant superintendent).

After 90 days of sifting through reams of documents; reviewing best practices in the education literature; talking with students, teachers, and stakeholders in the CAJ community; and having spirited discussions, the task force presented its report to Dr. Epps. The superintendent and school board approved the recommendations, which

included the following key (of many) components:

- Change the name of the school to C. A. Johnson Preparatory Academy (CAJPA) to reflect its emphasis on college readiness and academics.
- Provide opportunities for students to earn *dual credit* by taking college courses at no cost as part of a formal partnership with Benedict College.
- Require all incoming freshmen to participate in a four-week, academic-oriented residential *Summer Enrichment Program* housed on the college's campus.
- Require all students to take *college prep* and at least one AP course.
- Make available an *Enhancement Program* to all students who needed support with identified skill deficits.

On August 14, 2001, Superintendent Epps, Dr. David A. Swinton (president of Benedict College), and Mr. Vince Ford (chairman of the Richland One Board of School Commissioners), signed a formal memorandum of agreement to authorize a partnership between C. A. Johnson Preparatory Academy and Benedict College. Dr. Epps was excited about the new direction for the school, and he wanted that journey to begin under the leadership of a new principal. I thought my task was completed, but it had only just begun.

Throughout March of 2002, numerous applicants were screened, and several people interviewed for the principal's position at the new C. A. Johnson Preparatory Academy. Several candidates were presented to the superintendent, but he did not feel confident with any of them. In April 2002, Dr. Epps summoned me to his office again and said, "Jim, I really want C. A. Johnson Academy to be a success because that community deserves it. As a favor to me, would you serve as the principal for one year? No one knows more about the components of the academy than you do."

Dr. Epps' request caught me by surprise. I was quite comfortable working in the district office in a senior leadership position and as a member of the superintendent's cabinet. However, the thought of returning to my alma mater as its principal was somewhat intriguing, and like everyone else, I wanted what was best for the C. A. Johnson community. I accepted the superintendent's request and told him that I would lead the school for as long as it took to get it on the right track.

On July 1, 2002, I officially left the friendly confines of the John R. Stevenson Building or district office as an assistant superintendent to become the first principal of the inaugural C. A. Johnson Preparatory Academy. Although the challenge was daunting, so was my determination. Oh, by the way, there is one little tidbit that made the challenge even more daunting—this was my first principalship.

Having never been a principal, there were many things that I did not know about school finance, operations, curriculum, and instruction. Since I was a first-year principal, the South Carolina Department of Education offered me the opportunity to have a part-time mentor. This was strictly optional. Since I was not in denial and knew what I did not know, I accepted a mentor. To my good fortune, Mrs. Thomasenia Benson, a retired educator with over 35 years of experience, was assigned to me. She was known throughout the state for her leadership as the principal of a large predominantly black high school in Orangeburg, South Carolina.

Mrs. Benson and I bonded almost immediately. She would later tell me that she knew this was my first principalship, and she appreciated the fact that I was candid about the "things I did not know." Thus, we created an alliance that was characterized by mutual trust and respect for each other. This alliance was enhanced by the fact that both of us were *situational leaders*. As leaders, our approach to a situation was dictated by the amount of force that was needed. In Mrs. Benson's metaphorical words, "If the situation needs a soft, velvet hammer; we will use that. But if the situation needs a hard, steel hammer; we won't hesitate to use it, too."

Site Assessment

During my first week as principal in July 2002, students and faculty were still enjoying their summer vacation. This provided a great opportunity for me to develop a strategic plan to begin the work of reforming the school. The first order of business was to conduct a site assessment to determine the school's strengths and weaknesses, both real and perceived. This site assessment began with a comprehensive review of the school's data and culminated with a series of observations, conversations, and structured interviews.

Review of School Data

The first step toward getting to know my school was to review its data. For four days, I sat in my office and reviewed a plethora of documents related to the following:

- Demographics for students
- Demographics for teachers
- Student discipline data
- Financial records (budget)
- Teacher evaluations
- Standardized test data
- Standards for curriculum and instruction
- Report from the Southern Association of Colleges and Schools (SACS)
- Parent surveys

Rationale: *Before data-driven decisions can be made, the principal must be familiar with a school's data to determine areas of strengths and weaknesses. This enables the principal to determine the processes, procedures, practices, and personnel that need to be repaired, remediated, or replaced.*

Facility Walk-Through

During the six weeks before the students arrived on campus, I had the opportunity to familiarize myself with the school facility. With a notepad in hand, I initially toured the facility alone to make some cursory observations regarding the school's layout. A few days later, I asked Mrs. Benson and two assistant principals (APs) to join me for a more structured observation or walk-through of the facility. I also invited a fifth person to join us who knew more about the facility than anyone else—the head custodian, Mr. Trexton Black.

It was important for me to let Mr. Black know that I valued him as a member of my team. In fact, there were times when I invited him to join faculty meetings in his official role as the "chairman" of the custodial department. The walk-through led by Mr. Black was eye-opening to say the least. He pointed out several safety hazards and "hot spots" for inappropriate student activity that the APs, both of whom had been at the school for six years, were not aware existed.

For one thing, all the administrators' offices were located on the main floor of the three-story facility. Per Mr. Black, many students used this to their advantage to leave campus or create disputes with their peers in unsupervised areas. To the surprise and embarrassment of the APs, the head custodian was also aware of "things" that occurred in the classrooms.

When we entered one particular classroom, I noticed a loveseat and pole lamp were placed at the very front of the room. I asked one of the APs to explain why those items were in a classroom in which U. S. History was being taught. The AP proceeded to explain that the male teacher, who was very popular, would permit his "student of the week" to sit in the comfort of the loveseat during classroom instruction. The AP thought this was a great idea because the teacher said it "motivated" the students to earn that privilege.

At that point, I turned to the head custodian and said, "Mr. Black, if that chair could speak to me, what would it say?" Mr. Black shook his head and replied, "Dr. Taylor, I don't think you would want to know." I think everyone present got the gist of his reply. I had the loveseat and pole lamp removed immediately.

Throughout the entire site-assessment process, Mrs. Benson and I compiled separate and copious notes of our observations and interactions. We designated a time to meet weekly to compare our notes, which would be used to develop an "orientation" plan to present to faculty and staff during the week before the students arrived. The objective for that plan was to lay out the principal's expectations and the standard operating procedures and guidelines for conducting business at the school, which were teaching and learning.

The primary reason Mrs. Benson and I shared our copious noted during the weeks before the students arrived was to develop two comprehensive action plans—one for *operations* and one for *curriculum and instruction*. After those plans were written and posted in my conference room, they were implemented with fidelity throughout the entire school year.

Rationale: *The walk-through enabled me to become familiar with the facility, empower the head custodian, and surveil the campus for potential "hot spots" for possible inappropriate student behavior.*

Structured Conversations (Administrators)

The administrative team I inherited consisted of three assistant principals and a curriculum coordinator. The superintendent had authorized me to displace 10 members of the faculty, which could include any member of my administrative team. After a review of the administrators' personnel files, I had a one-hour structured conversation with each one of them. My goal was to assess their individual depth of knowledge, commitment to the principles of the academy, interpersonal skills, trustworthiness, and leadership style. Moreover, I wanted to gauge their perception of areas at the school that were exemplary and those that needed improvement.

Based on the structured conversations, I could determine which areas the administrators perceived as needing improvement. They seemed to agree that teacher apathy, student discipline, a high rate of absenteeism for students and staff, and a lack of school pride were major areas of concern. While none of the administrators had what I would call a "wow-factor", they seemed adequate. I was careful not to make a hasty decision to displace any them and allow valuable "institutional knowledge" to leave the building that could be used to improve the school.

Besides, as part of the approved proposal for the academy, I was permitted to hire a "rising star" as my dean of academics, Mr. Thomas Rivers. While at CAJPA, Mrs. Benson, SRO William Hilton, Mr. Rivers, and Mrs. Rachell Wallace, my administrative assistant, emerged as my primary fiduciary or trust agents. Their presence eased any anxieties I had about keeping the administrative team I inherited.

Rationale: *The primary responsibility of an assistant principal is to implement the principal's vision and school's mission. I needed to know whether my administrators, either wittingly or unwittingly, grasped that principle.*

Structured Conversations (Teachers)

The importance of having good teachers cannot be overstated. Due to negative perceptions, many good teachers in Richland School District One had absolutely no desire to teach at C. A. Johnson. Thus, the district often contracted with outside agencies to secure foreign teachers with H-1-B visas to teach at C. A. Johnson. When C. A. Johnson Preparatory Academy opened in 2002, 11 of the 46 certified teachers at the school had H-1-B visas to teach. Although the student population was 99 percent black (there was one white student enrolled), the faculty was highly diverse. This created an undeniable student-teacher culture gap.

Mrs. Benson and I divided the list of teachers and interviewed each one separately for 30 minutes. We asked each teacher seven open-ended questions that were designed to assess their knowledge of the subject matter they taught, views regarding multiculturalism, and strategies they used to maximize instruction. At the end of three days of structured interviews, we discussed our findings and decided to transfer eight teachers, one guidance counselor, and one media specialist. With those transfers, a clear message reverberated throughout the CAJPA faculty, there would be no excuses accepted for ineffective classroom instruction.

Rationale: *Through structured face-to-face conversations, a principal can get an initial snapshot of a teacher's communication skills, knowledge, and passion for teaching.*

Structured Conversations (Students)

The best way to find out what happens in classrooms and on a school's campus daily is fairly simple—ask the students. One week before all students arrived, I invited six student leaders to meet with me in my conference room for a discussion over lunch. I selected the student body president, junior class president, and captain of the football team to attend. Each assistant principal selected one "average" student to participate. Ultimately, I had three boys and three girls and a fairly representative cross-section of the student body.

Our discussion was easily the most rich and informative one I had with any entity or group prior to the first day of school. The students were candid and insightful. They really appreciated the fact that I, the principal, was interested in hearing their voices. Throughout the luncheon, I looked for an opportunity to respond with immediate action to a concern to demonstrate my willingness to make CAJPA a better school. Then, it happened; the football captain, James Heatley, expressed a concern.

James indicated that the football team had the same pregame meal for the past two years – hot dogs or hamburgers, salad, mashed potatoes, rolls, and milk or tea. I thought he was kidding but he wasn't. When I investigated this allegation, the athletic director (AD) confirmed James' concern and blamed the booster club for not providing sufficient revenue to fully support the football team. I was appalled by his explanation and lack of concern for the welfare of the student-athletes. Since this proved to be typical of his apathy and nonchalant attitude, the AD was relieved of his duties the following year.

As for the football team, they noticed a change in pre-game meal the very next week before they donned their gear for the annual Sports-a-Rama. This was an annual event in which high school football teams in the Columbia area kickoff the season by playing two quarters against a rival. On the evening prior to the game, I sat with the CAJPA football players in the school's cafeteria and ate a high-quality pregame meal with them that did not include hotdogs or hamburgers. The kids were ecstatic.

Unexpectedly, this small gesture laid the foundation for my four-year tenure as the principal of CAJPA. First and foremost, the students realized that I was willing to listen to their concerns and act as needed. In other words, I cared. Equally as important, the six student-leaders I met with in my conference room, along with the entire football team, served as my best and most credible ambassadors. They took it upon themselves to tell their peers that the new principal is "okay."

Rationale: On Day One, it is essential for students to feel as if their voices are heard and their concerns matter. This lays the foundation for a school-wide climate of mutual respect.

Informal Observations (Operations)

After the students arrived, it was important to get a feel for the climate in the school. Several questions needed to be answered. How do students interact with each other? How do teachers interact with students? Do students take pride in their school? Do teachers take pride in their school? One way to answer these and other questions is through structured observations.

On the first day of school, I had a 30-minute assembly with each of the four grade levels of students—freshmen, sophomores, juniors, and seniors. During those assemblies, I introduced myself and laid out my expectations for all students. It was important for the students to know that I was their leader, and I did so with a stern (but not over-the-top) demeanor.

As a situational leader, I opted to use my stern "steel hammer" to get their attention. As several weeks passed, I started to use my "velvet hammer" more frequently. It is very important to know that it is much more effective to start with the steel (stern) one and then progress to the velvet (warm) one. Going from velvet to steel is risky because that tends to confuse students and staff.

Over the course of the next few days, it was important for the students to "see" me and vice versa. I knew the school had a reputation for having student-on-student conflicts in the form of excessive fighting. A situation I observed while patrolling the halls when students were en route to their classes still resonates with me. While accompanied by one of my APs, I noticed a group of about eight males leaning against a wall and glaring at another group of males leaning against a wall across from them. When I asked the AP what was going on, his reply stunned me. He said, "This wall (pointing to it) belongs to the Bloods and that one (pointing to it) belongs to the Folks. Right now, they are 'mean mugging' each other."

That scenario in the hallway spoke volumes to the climate that existed at the school and the need for immediate change. As a rule of thumb, it is always a good practice to correct student misbehavior immediately. Both the students and AP were shocked when I uttered these stern words in the hall that day, "These walls do not belong to anyone in this school. These are my walls!"

Yes, there was a gang-related faction in the school that needed to be addressed quickly; otherwise, the Folks and the Bloods would run the school, not me. Over the course of the next few days, I noticed a lot of gang members wearing their so-called colors. The Folks wore black and Bloods wore red.

Fortunately, the Columbia Police Department had assigned an experienced resource officer to the school, Officer William Hilton. Although Officer Hilton, who was a graduate of CAJ, was an expert in gang lore, the school's administration had never tapped into his expertise. He indicated that he felt like an outsider whose only responsibility was to break up fights. Officer Hilton's duties and responsibilities quickly expanded to include being a law-enforcement counselor and a law-enforcement educator.

Rationale: *During school, the principal is the parent for each child*—in loco parentis. *Thus, as the parent of all students at CAJPA, it was important for them to feel that I was always roaming, nurturing, protecting, and correcting them.*

Informal Observations (Students and Teachers)

Teachers perform the single most important duty of any entity in a school——teaching. There is no way for a principal to know what is going on in the classrooms unless she or he makes routine visits. During the entire 180 days of a school year, my goal was to make daily visits to classrooms to observe teaching and learning. As principal, it was my responsibility to set the tone for teaching and learning during the first week of school.

The initial reaction to my informal classroom observations from teachers and students was one of suspicion. Eventually, they grew accustomed to my presence and looked forward to my visits. These observations were informal because I did not have a notepad with me. I would, however, take mental notes and write contemporaneous memos as needed. My primary purpose was to let the teachers and students know that I valued teaching and learning, and nothing was more important than for my students to get a quality education.

Although my routine 20-minute unannounced classroom observations were informal, they were highly productive. My observations gave me the opportunity to interact with my students in a smaller setting, and of course, I got to see my teachers in action. In many ways, my presence in the classrooms stimulated the phenomenon psychologists refer to as *social facilitation*, which is a tendency for others to perform well-learned tasks more effectively in the presence of others. During these classroom observations, I became the "others" and the "well-learned tasks" were teaching and learning.

Rationale: *As the instructional leader of a school, it is vitally important for a principal to embrace that responsibility and implement a hands-on approach to teaching and learning.*

Informal Conversations (Students and Teachers)

Invaluable information regarding a school can be obtained through simple and informal conversations with the key players—students and teachers. More often than not, their perceptions translate into facts that can be used for planning. Through informal chats with teachers, I was able to determine what additional resources were needed to improve teaching and learning at CAJPA, as well as identify the students they perceived as most disruptive.

Student behavior dictates a school's climate. Teaching and learning cannot occur in the middle of chaos and disruption. Research indicates that most students go to school to learn, which was certainly true at CAJPA. With the help of concerned students, I was able to identify the leaders of the school's gang factions and the ideology they espoused. This pivotal information was used to develop strategies to improve the school's climate.

Rationale: *Relationships are built through informal conversations. And those relationships can be used to create a positive and safe climate conducive to teaching and learning.*

Guiding Principles

Admittedly, I am not a fan of mission statements. They tend to be rather esoteric, use the same educational buzz words, and no one remembers them. When I asked my administrative team to recite the mission statement from the previous school year, none of them could remember it. However, it is important for students, staff, and stakeholders to understand a principal's goals for a school.

During my tenure at CAJPA, we had a set of three guiding principles that governed everything we did. All students and staff members could recite those guiding principles without hesitation. They were captured in the acronym BIC:

Build community trust.

Improve student achievement.

Create an environment conducive to teaching and learning.

Whenever a proposal or a written request was submitted to me for approval, it had to include a comprehensive statement with an answer to this simple question: Which guiding principle(s) is aligned with your request?

Rationale: *Proverbs 29:18: Where there is no vision, the people perish.*

Action Plans

After weeks of gathering and analyzing data through a series of observations, conversations, and reading documents, it was time to develop action plans to transform CAJPA from a low-performing high school to a high-performing academy. Those plans involved strategies that included:

- School climate
- Curriculum
- Classroom instruction
- Community relations

School Climate

If C. A. Johnson was to make the successful transition toward becoming an academy, it had to feel and look like one. A school riddled with gang activity, low expectations, and pockets of unprofessionalism within the faculty had neither the right feel nor the right look. To my displeasure, none of the male faculty members wore a tie and denim jeans were the garment of choice for many female teachers. The actual action plan that was developed to change the dreadful climate at C. A. Johnson is presented in Table 14.

The four action plans were professionally printed on posters and prominently displayed on my conference room wall. During each weekly meeting with my administrative team, we reviewed our progress with each plan. Most of the action steps in Action Plan #1 occurred before students arrived on campus. It was important to have our plan developed and ready for implementation. Otherwise, the students would continue to implement their plan, which was to perpetuate an atmosphere of chaos and confusion.

Table 14

Action Plan #1: School Climate

GOAL: Create the climate of an academy conducive to teaching and learning.

Action Step	Assigned to	Due Date	Date Completed
Have a faculty meeting to discuss the Professional Code of Conduct for Staff.	Principal	July 2002	July 2002
Revise the Student Discipline Code of Conduct to clearly outline expectations.	Assistant Principal #2	July 2002	July 2002
Have an assembly with each grade level to review the Student Discipline Code of Conduct.	Principal APs	August 2002	August 2002
Meet with gang leaders.	Principal and SRO	September 2002	Ongoing
Establish the Principal's Student Advisory Council.	Principal and Secretary	October 2002	Ongoing
Establish the Principal's Community Advisory Council.	Principal Admin Assistant	October 2002	Ongoing
Develop and implement an Advisor-Advisee Program for schoolwide implementation.	Assistant Principal #3	October 2002	October 2002
Schedule at least two mandatory workshops for Teachers (re: Classroom Management).	Assistant Principal #1	December 2002	November 2002
Discuss expectations for classroom management during faculty meetings.	Principal and APs	Ongoing	Ongoing

Perhaps the most important climate-altering partnership we forged was with the gang leaders. After the gang leaders were identified, I met with them (three Bloods and three Folks) at least twice a month. (See Step #4 in Action Plan #1.) They truly embraced the idea that I wanted them to help me create and maintain a safe environment at OUR school—C. A. Johnson Preparatory Academy. My administrators really had an eye-opening experience when they realized that the leader of the Folks was a small and unassuming student named Raheem, and the leader of the Bloods was a star all-around athlete named Chris.

Within a matter of weeks, the gang activity at CAJPA was practically nonexistent. The gang leaders had agreed to a truce that was in effect from arrival to dismissal of school. That truce was honored during my entire four years at CAJPA. Beneath the tough façade that some students like gang members project, they are typical teenagers who readily comply with expectations that come from nurturing and caring adults, especially when those expectations come from the principal.

Curriculum

Several components of the superintendent's plan to reform C. A. Johnson focused on strengthening the school's written and taught curriculums. The action plan shown in Table 15 was developed and implemented to improve and reform the curriculum. The initial focus was directed toward all incoming freshmen. They were required to participate in a four-week summer enrichment program to prepare them for the rigors of the curricula.

Over 90 percent of the incoming freshmen participated in the summer enrichment program. This gave me, the administrative team, and several teachers the opportunity to build meaningful relationships with the incoming freshman class before school began in mid-August. Moreover, during that four weeks, each student was given pre-assessments that were used to develop an individual Prescriptive Educational Plan (PEP). The students lauded the benefits of the program, which proved to be one of the seminal features of C. A. Johnson's transformation from a traditional urban high school to an academic-oriented academy.

Table 15

Action Plan #2: Curriculum

GOAL: Create a rigorous, relevant curriculum with "supports" to ensure that all students receive a high-quality education.

Action Step	Assigned to	Due Date	Date Completed
1. Visit the middle schools in the CAJPA cluster to inform their graduating eighth graders about enrolling in the mandatory Summer Enrichment Academy at Benedict College.	Principal and Dean of Academics	April 2002	April 2002
2. Develop and implement the first Benedict Summer Enrichment Academy for incoming freshmen.	Dean of Academics	April 2001	July 2002
3. Develop a master schedule to ensure that all freshmen will have a 90-minute block of English and Math.	Guidance Department	July 2002	July 2002
4. Identify all students who will need developmental education (DE) classes and place them accordingly.	Guidance Department	June 2002	August 2002
5. Confer with Benedict College to identify the courses that will be offered for dual credit.	Curriculum Coordinator	June 2002	July 2002

Action Step	Assigned to	Due Date	Date Completed
6. Arrange for all students to take College Prep, AP, and/or Dual Credit courses at some point.	Guidance Department	August 2002	Ongoing
7. Develop a process that will be used for all twelfth graders to complete and present a mandatory Senior Thesis.	Curriculum Coordinator and English Department	December 2002	January 2003

The essence of the reformed curriculum was to challenge students in the classroom, while providing *supports* or safety nets to ensure their success. It was like teaching the students to swim in deep water while providing them with lifejackets and a lifeguard within several feet. The academic supports for the students at CAJPA included an advisor program (i.e., each student was assigned an adult mentor), afterschool tutoring, Saturday tutoring, developmental education (DE) classes, and opportunities to recover lost credits via an online computer program.

The ultimate goal was for each student to take pride in becoming a CAJPA scholar. As such, those students would take a series of college prep, AP, and dual credit courses. In addition, Benedict College offered a full academic scholarship to any CAJPA student who completed at least four of the college's dual credit courses with a minimum grade point average of 3.0.

Classroom Instruction

The importance of engaging students in classroom instruction cannot be overstated. An engaged student is learning, while a disengaged student is not learning. When I arrived, the faculty at CAJPA overall could have been described as somewhat passionate but ineffective. A lot of the ineffectiveness was due to a huge culture gap between the students and teachers. Although the student body was 99 percent black, the faculty resembled the United Nations. Among the 46 certified teachers, three were from Romania, three from India, two from Lithuania, two from Nigeria, one from Colombia (South America), one from Kenya, and one from Ghana.

The challenge was obvious. With a faculty that included 13 foreign, 8 white, and 25 black teachers, a strategy was needed to bridge the culture gap between the students and their teachers. As indicated in Action Plan #3, ongoing strategies and comprehensive professional development were implemented to assist the teachers with student engagement. (See Table 16.) Dr. Jan Witty, director of Benedict College's Teacher Education Program, and Ms. Nikki Mouton, an education consultant, helped to close this culture gap by providing comprehensive professional development in culturally responsive pedagogy to all CAJPA faculty.

Table 16

Action Plan #3: Instruction

GOAL: Provide culturally relevant and engaging instruction in all classrooms.

Action Step	Assigned to	Due Date	Date Completed
1. Provide comprehensive professional development in culturally responsive pedagogy for all teachers.	Assistant Principal #3	August 2002	Ongoing
2. Develop a form to use for recording classroom observations.	Principal's Mentor	September 2002	September 2002

Action Step	Assigned to	Due Date	Date Completed
3. Develop and implement a schedule whereby all assistant principals and the dean of academics will conduct weekly formal and informal classroom observations.	Principal's Mentor	September 2002	September 2002
4. Develop and disseminate to all teachers an evidence-based manual titled *Effective Instructional Strategies at C. A. Johnson Preparatory Academy*.	Department Chairs and Curriculum Coordinator	December 2002	November 2002
5. Ensure that all department chairpersons use the manual as part of their discussions with teachers during their biweekly departmental meetings.	Curriculum Coordinator	January 2003	January 2003

By October 2002, there was a noticeable connection between the teachers and students. This connection even extended beyond the classroom. The teacher from Nigeria had created a soccer team; the teacher from Colombia had become the assistant junior varsity cheerleader coach; one of the white teachers assisted with the marching band; and one of the teachers from India had started a math club. Slowly but surely, CAJPA was becoming an all-inclusive family and everyone was involved in teaching and learning.

Community Relations

One of the three guiding principles for CAJPA was to "build community trust." Findings in the research literature indicate that when schools, parents, and communities work together to support teaching and learning, students tend to attend school more regularly, stay in school longer, and enroll in higher level programs. Action Plan #4 was developed to create those outcomes at CAJPA. (See Table 17.)

Table 17

Action Plan #4: Community and Parent Relations

GOAL: Build positive relationships with community and parent stakeholders to share in the responsibility of educating the students at CAJPA.

Action Step	Assigned to	Due Date	Date Completed
1. Hold a forum at the school to introduce the administrative team and make the community and stakeholders aware (via a PowerPoint and video) of the school's new direction.	Principal Admin Team Secretary	September 2002	October 2002
2. Create a parent-community advisory council to meet with the principal and administrative team monthly.	Assistant Principal #2 and Administrative Assistant	September 2002	Ongoing
3. Revise and improve the school's website to include a Principal's Newsletter page to provide school-related updates to students, parents, staff, and stakeholders.	Technology Team	September 2002	Ongoing

The parents and community embraced the opportunity to become a part of the rebirth of C. A. Johnson. Like all parents across America, the parents of the students at CAJPA wanted their children to receive a quality education in a safe environment. Once they were convinced (by actions, not words!) of my passion to serve *in loco parentis* to their children, the parents and community gave me and my agenda their full support. The action steps shown in Action Plan #4 paved the way for that outcome.

Mission Accomplished

Most states conduct annual evaluations of their schools based on climate ratings (which are determined by parent and student surveys) and student achievement scores (which are determined by outcomes on standardized assessments). The best way to gauge the success of the rebirth of C. A. Johnson is to review outcomes in school climate and student achievement across a four-year period. Both qualitative and quantitative measures were used to assist with drawing conclusions.

School Climate

Prior to becoming an academy, C. A. Johnson had the most per capita fights of any school in the entire school district. On average, there were slightly over 21 major fights in the school per year from 1998 through 2001. Many of those fights involved multiple students and could be considered brawls. The culture of fighting at the school decreased dramatically through the ongoing implementation of Action Plan #1.

During the first year (2002–2003) of the plan, there were a total of seven fights in the school. By the fourth year (2005–2006), that number had gradually decreased to a total of zero. That is not a typo—there were no fights at C. A. Johnson Preparatory Academy during the 2005–2006 school year. The school had become one of the safest and most inviting havens for teaching and learning in the entire Richland County area.

Two key factors were directly related to the transformation the school's climate. The first factor was the principal setting the tone for all staff having an *unconditional positive regard* or caring attitude for all students, regardless of their background, socio-economic status, academic ranking, gender, or appearance. At CAJPA, all students were treated with respect.

An attitude of unconditional positive regard cannot be faked; it must be genuine. Most teenagers in urban schools, at least in Richland County, are quite adept at judging whether an adult is sincerely concerned about their health, safety, and welfare. At CAJPA, meaningful relationships were built between students and adult staff. All full-time members of the staff, including the custodians, secretaries, bookkeeper, campus monitors, etc., were encouraged to "adopt" a student to mentor. Through this process, coupled with the advisor-advisee program, each student on the campus had an adult advocate or mentor.

A powerful testament to the change that occurred in the climate at CAJPA can be summarized in a student-on-student interaction I witnessed during the second semester of the 2003–2004 year. One morning a male student from another school entered the building accompanied by his mother to enroll as a transfer. The new student wore a blue bandana and had another one hanging from the back pocket of his jeans. Without hesitation, two male CAJPA students approached him in a nonthreatening manner and said, "Hey, man, you need to take off that doo-rag because we don't wear them in here. You can put it back on after school."

The new student complied with the request. The keyword the students used in that incident was "we". This was a clear indication that the CAJPA student body had begun to take ownership of the school's climate, and they embraced the direction the school was moving. It was their school and they felt comfortable in it, and they were not going to let anyone disrupt their haven for teaching, learning, and safety.

Academic Achievement

Like the phoenix in Greek mythology, student achievement at CAJPA rose from the ashes. The first indication of improvement occurred in 2003 when the South Carolina State Department of Education released a report on how each of the state's 198 high schools fared on the South

Carolina High School Exit Exam. As indicated in Table 18, C. A. Johnson Preparatory Academy had the sixth highest gain score (i.e., improvement over the previous year's scores) among all high schools in the state.

Table 18

Exit Exam (First Attempt)

Top Gains Among South Carolina's High School 2003

Rank	School	Percent Free or Reduced Lunch	Number Tested	Gain
1.	Jonesville High	50.8	51	+24.8
2.	Branchville High	35.3	25	+21.7
3.	Scott's Branch High	86.9	79	+21.5
4.	Wade Hampton High	46.8	146	+17.2
5.	Bowman High	78.6	37	+16.8
6.	**C. A. Johnson Preparatory Academy**	**69.8**	**113**	**+16.0**
7.	The Phoenix Center	80.0	9	+14.4
8.	Crescent High	41.5	142	+13.2

Rank	School	Percent Free or Reduced Lunch	Number Tested	Gain
8.	Crescent High	41.5	142	+13.2
9.	Lewisville High	31.7	83	+12.9
10.	Carvers Bay	71.8	113	+12.6
11.	Lincoln High	74.1	20	+11.9
12.	Chester High	41.4	171	+11.4
	STATE'S AVERAGE	**26.9**	N/A	**+0.2**

Source: South Carolina State Department of Education.

    Scores on the Scholastic Aptitude Test (SAT) offered another measure of students' academic performance. Once again, CAJPA distinguished itself on a standardized test of student achievement. The SAT scores for students at CAJPA improved from 840 in 2004 to 935 in 2005. As indicated in Table 19, this 95-point gain ranked fourth among all high schools in South Carolina. These scores provide evidence that by the third year under the tenets of the academy concepts, CAJPA was on a clear upward trajectory and in the middle of a significant turnaround.

Table 19

SAT Scores for South Carolina High Schools 2005

Rank	School	Gain
1.	Mid Carolina High	+128
2.	Woodland High	+110
3.	Newberry Senior High	+103
4.	**C. A. Johnson Preparatory Academy**	**+95**
5.	Darlington High	+94
5.	Lamar High	+94
7.	Septima Clark Academy	+90
8.	Buford High	+85
9.	Calhoun County High	+85
10.	Branchville High	+81
11.	Crescent High	+81
12.	Williston-Elko High	+75
13.	Lincoln High	+74
14.	Woodmont High	+68
15.	Jaspar County	+66
15.	Jonesville High	+66

Source: South Carolina State Department of Education.

If teaching is the most important thing inside the classroom, then leadership is the most important thing outside the classroom. After a few episodes of discord and disagreement, the administrative team at CAJPA functioned as a unit to implement the principal's guiding principles of BIC. There were many valuable lessons learned about building trust, having high expectations for all students and staff, and exerting the leadership needed to create an enterprise for teaching and learning. The three assistant principals (Bobby Cunningham, Francina Shack, and Isaac McClinton) and assistant administrator (Mickey Pringle) learned those lessons well and became principals of high schools within three years after my departure from CAJPA.

The "rising star" I hired to serve as the dean of academics did not disappoint me; he learned his lessons extremely well and exceeded all expectations. Thomas Rivers left CAJPA one year after I left; earned his doctorate in Education Administration and Leadership from the University of South Carolina; was recognized as the South Carolina Assistant Principal of the Year in 2015; and currently serves as the principal of a high-performing middle school in Lexington, South Carolina.

The most compelling testimony to the rebirth of C. A. Johnson High School would be to examine the class of 2006. The students in that class were freshmen when the academy concept was implemented, which gave them the opportunity to complete their secondary education under that framework—as well as the structure provided by the four action plans—during their entire four years of high school. Ninety percent of the graduates of the class of 2006 continued their education in either a two-year or four-year institution. Seven notable members of that class include Katherine Myers (valedictorian), Amber Hendrix (salutatorian), Chad Washington, LaKesa McGraw, Maurice Lindsay, Stephanie Jones, and Demetrius Bouttry.

Katherine and Amber still reside in Richland County and both are prominent attorneys in the community. Chad, a star athlete during his four years at CAJPA, has a master's degree and currently serves as the athletics director at an HBCU. LaKesa has a master's degree and currently works in the corporate sector as a director of human resources management. Maurice has an associate's degree and has published a book about the history of religion in America. Stephanie is an officer in the United States Armed Forces. Demetrius, a former gang leader, has a bachelor's degree and is now a police officer protecting and serving citizens in the C. A. Johnson community.

Chapter Summary

When a mother gives birth to her first child, the newborn does not emerge with a set of written best practices for child-rearing attached to it. The mother must rely on her "leadership" and her life-experiences to become an effective parent. However, the key factor in the parenting process is love. Despite her level of education or socioeconomic status, when a mother sincerely loves her child, she will likely be a successful parent.

This same principle holds true in educational leadership. When I became a first-year principal, C. A. Johnson Preparatory Academy was my "newborn child." As the school's leader, it was incumbent upon me to make decisions that would positively impact the lives of my children. Surprisingly, that daunting task became a wonderful educational experience for everyone simply because of that key factor—I fell in love with the students at CAJPA.

As the new principal or *in loco parentis*, it was important for me to realize that each child was unique and a one-size-fits-all approach to "childrearing" would be counterproductive. To understand the uniqueness of children, imagine that each child was a tire for a vehicle. Some tires fit a car, a truck, a van, or even a bicycle. Also, because tires come in different sizes, they require various amounts of pounds per square inch (psi) to inflate. When I arrived at CAJPA in 2002, many of my "tires" were unwanted and deflated. It became my job to determine the amount of psi (or personal student intervention) each child needed to become fully functional.

In 2001, the South Carolina Department of Education had dubbed C. A. Johnson a failing school. My job was to provide the leadership needed to erase that failing grade and make it an A. The letter "A" is significant because it captures the three-pronged process that my team and I used to transform the school—*Atmosphere*, *Academics*, and *Attitude*.

The *atmosphere* refers to the school climate. CAJPA was a school riddled with chaos and fighting. Changing the climate or atmosphere was the first order of business because teaching and learning cannot occur in a chaotic or unsafe environment. The atmosphere at CAJPA was changed via a series of action plans, and most importantly, by building trust that extended from the principal's office to the classroom.

Academics at CAJPA occurred in the most important place at the school—the classroom. Students were challenged in the classroom through a rigorous curriculum that included mandatory college prep, advanced placement, and dual credit courses. Students lost their fear of failure due to supports that were provided to ensure their success in the classroom.

The *attitude* at the school change dramatically because all students were expected to be scholars. The teachers received extensive training in culturally responsive teaching strategies, which helped to elevate their level of high expectations for students. The administrators routinely praised teachers when they demonstrated high-level instructional skills, and students were routinely recognized and rewarded for their leadership and academic accomplishments.

The four years I served as principal of CAJPA were the most pleasant of my 40-year career in education. Again, I cannot express how important it is for principals to have a strong positive regard for their students. I became very attached to my students, and they knew it. By working together, we recaptured the viability of a historically black school, which was once a beacon of the educational light that illuminated in South Carolina during the separate-but-equal era of the 1960s and 1970s.

Part IV

NOW WHAT?

CHAPTER 10

Conclusion

The purpose of this book was to remind America of her checkered educational past, which should remind us to develop a more effective educational system for the future. A truly sad episode in that past was the plight of black citizens and their struggle to gain equal access to K–12 public and higher education in America. That sad episode was a story of oppression and suppression, which occurred during the Jim Crow era when young blacks were taught to live in fear of and subservience to whites. Despite an eventual repeal of the Jim Crow system of *de jure* oppression, various forms of *de facto* educational suppression of blacks persist today.

In the prologue of this book, I gave the reader a personal glimpse of what America's educational system looked like through the eyes of a black child during the 1950s, 1960s, and 1970s. My experience as a student in an all-black separate-but-equal elementary school in the 1950s was actually quite memorable due to the nurturing black teachers who shielded me and other black children from the evils of a segregated society.

That shield of protection was removed when I entered secondary school and college. I experienced my first sting of disparate treatment when I attended a predominantly white middle school in the early 1960s. All my teachers were white females, and most of them had low expectations regarding my ability to compete with my white classmates. My fight with these low expectations continued when I was among the first wave of African American students to integrate the University of South Carolina in 1966. Discrimination against blacks was a reality in both K–12 public and higher education in America during the twentieth century.

After decades of turmoil and racial discrimination, what does the future hold for children of color in America's educational system in the twenty-first century? Will reforms in education create a utopian system whereby schools will have high expectations for children based on the color of their blood and not the color of their skin? What will it take for real substantive changes to occur in America's education system? Will the twenty-first century be characterized by a period of reform or a period of regression in both public and higher education?

The importance of leadership in any country or organization can never be overstated. People in organizations generally follow their leader's agenda whether it is destructive or constructive. This may explain why Germany embraced Adolph Hitler's destructive and race-based Nazi ideology in the 1930s. One of Hitler's most infamous quotes was, "If you tell a big enough lie and tell it frequently enough, it will be believed." Even in America today, white supremacists follow a destructive and racist neo-Nazi agenda espoused by their leader, Richard Spencer.

When change occurred in our educational system in the 1960s, the political leadership in America made a strong commitment to provide equal opportunities for all children, regardless of their race or socioeconomic circumstance. Presidents John F. Kennedy and Lyndon B. Johnson, in addition to the Supreme Court, exerted leadership at the highest levels of our government to dismantle an American educational system that was blemished by a history of racial segregation and discrimination. Because of leadership at the top, African Americans like Barack Obama (first black elected president of the *Harvard Law Review* in 1990), Dr. Mae C. Jemison (first black woman astronaut in 1992), Maurice Ashley (first black International Grandmaster in chess in 1999), and Dr. Condoleezza Rice (first black woman appointed U.S. Secretary of State in 2005) all had access to integrated public schools in the 1970s.

To put the notion of educational reform into a metaphorical perspective, think of it in terms of having to paint a room in a house. A simple but effective approach for completing this task could entail a four-step process of *inspection, selection, preparation,* and *implementation*. (See Figure 1.) The first step (inspection) would involve looking at the room to determine its dimensions and assess it for possible damage. The second step (selection) would involve choosing an appropriate quality, quantity, and color of paint. The third step (preparation) would involve moving furniture, sanding the walls and masking them with tape, and spreading a drop cloth to protect the floors. The final step (implementation) would be to use a quality brush to apply the paint onto the walls.

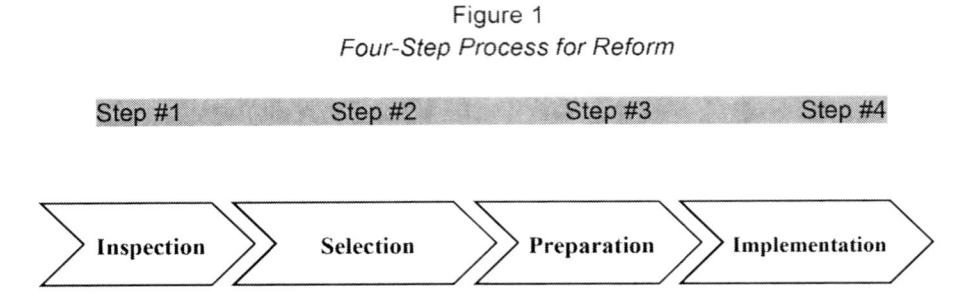

Figure 1
Four-Step Process for Reform

Step #1	Step #2	Step #3	Step #4
Inspection	Selection	Preparation	Implementation

This four-step process could be used as an approach or guide to reform the eroding system of education in America today. This book has taken us through the first two steps of the four-step process. Parts I and II chronicle a comprehensive, historical <u>inspection</u> of America's educational system. These two parts provide a lens that enables us to see the scope of past failures and assess the damage that was done to children. Part III takes us through the second step of the process—<u>selection</u>. Metaphorically speaking, this part tells us the quantity, quality, and color of the "reform paint" needed to improve the "education-walls" in America. In other words, Part III (or Step 2) elucidates action strategies (e.g., nondiscriminatory policies, culturally responsive pedagogy, college affordability, etc.) that are needed to reform our system of public and higher education.

America is currently stuck in a socio-political quagmire that is impeding our ability to transition to Step #3 The vitriol in today's politics is increasing because the nation's political parties are becoming increasingly more divided along demographic lines of race, income, religion, and gender identification. Physical and social differences have made it easy for people to disagree with and vilify members of the opposing party.

This became evident on June 14, 2017, when top Republican Congressman Steve Scalise and four of his colleagues were shot and wounded while practicing for a congressional baseball game in Alexandria, Virginia. The gunman in that incident was killed after a shootout with law enforcement officers. He was identified as a 66-year-old native of Illinois, and his Facebook account was filled with anti-Republican posts and rhetoric.

Another episode of social and politically charged divisiveness occurred in Virginia two months later. On August 12, 2017, hundreds of white nationalists, members of the Ku Klux Klan, and neo-Nazis gathered in Charlottesville to protest the removal of a statue honoring Confederate General Robert E. Lee. The white nationalists, who came from communities coast-to-coast, marched through the University of Virginia's campus wielding torches, dressed in paramilitary uniforms, waving confederate flags, brandishing weapons, and chanting their neo-Nazi slogan "blood and soil."

This march was a sad day in America's history and exposed the level of hatred that still exists today. When counter-protestors assembled to express their opposition to the neo-Nazi ideology of the white nationalists, violence erupted. One person was killed, and 19 others were injured after a car plowed through a group of counter-protestors.

Given the current social and political landscape, is America ready to transition to Step #3, <u>preparation</u>, of the four-step process to reform her system of secondary and higher education? As indicated by the black or shaded chevrons in Figure 2, this book has taken us through the first two steps by providing a historical account of past failures and offering solutions to resolve them. The unshaded or white chevrons signify the two remaining steps that need action. At this point, the only thing needed to propel America into Step #3 is leadership at the top levels of our government. The divisive and volatile political landscape in the 1960s did not prevent Presidents Kennedy and Johnson, as well as the Supreme Court, from exerting the leadership needed to desegregate schools and create equal opportunities for all children of color.

Figure 2
Four-Step Process for Reform
(Steps Completed)

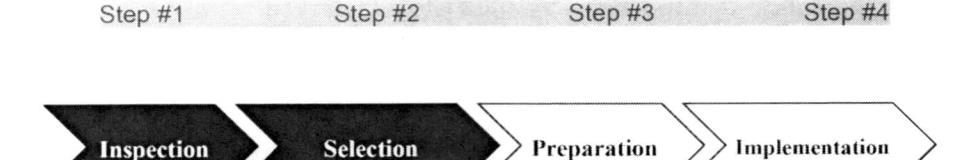

Step #1 — Step #2 — Step #3 — Step #4

Inspection › Selection › Preparation › Implementation

As we near the end of this book, there is one indisputable conclusion that can be drawn: America's educational system is stagnant and needs to be reformed. Despite increasing diversity, the system continues to have difficulty engaging and teaching children of color. The socio-educational continuum for black children in America's educational system moved from separate-and-unequal (*de jure* segregation) during the first part of the twentieth century to desegregation during the middle part of the twentieth century to equal-but-unwanted (*de facto* discrimination) that began during the latter part of the twentieth century.

Although children of color are fundamentally included in all the nation's institutions of public and higher education, America's educational system in the twenty-first century is continuing to sink into a state of relapse. This relapse is characterized by a rise in racism and low expectations for children of color. Many of these children sit in classrooms virtually invisible to teachers who often ignore them for various reasons related to preexisting stereotypes and biases. Children who are equal but feel unwanted in the classroom are more at risk for having low academic achievement and high rates of out-of-school suspensions.

As recently as September 26, 2017, a study conducted by Hua-Yu Cherng of New York University indicates that many teachers have difficulty establishing meaningful relationships with teenagers of color and children of immigrants. Cherng concluded, "Teachers' relationships are hugely important for all students, but particularly so for groups that are marginalized. Yet, the students who could benefit from relationships with their teachers are the ones that have the least access to strong teacher-student relationships." This is more evidence of the relapse of education for unwanted children in America.

In the face of this relapse in our nation's educational system, this is the central question: Is the current leadership at the top levels of government willing and capable of leading America into Step #4 or the <u>implementation</u> phase of educational reform? I have my doubts. It is difficult to determine current President Donald Trump's position on either public or higher education. During his campaign, Mr. Trump questioned whether the federal government should even have a department of education. He seems to change his opinion on public education based on his audience. For the most part, President Trump is in favor of providing families with vouchers to select a public, private, or charter school of their choice.

Two key members of the president's administration also hold this policy position. When he served as governor of Indiana, Vice President Mike Pence championed school choice and favored the federal government having a limited role in public education. Current U. S. Secretary of Education Betsy DeVos led a movement to privatize public education in Michigan, and she was the main force behind the spread of charter schools in that state. In fact, most of the charter schools in Michigan have recorded student test scores in reading and math below the state average.

It is also hard to pinpoint Donald Trump's position on higher education. Even though he promised to provide additional funding to HBCUs, his proposed budget for 2018 did not reflect that support. Moreover, his proposal to address student loan debt was equally as confusing and disappointing. Again, it will take strong and decisive leadership from the White House if any substantive reform is to occur in our nation's education system.

There can be no doubt that educational reform is not a priority under the current president's agenda. Therefore, the chances of any substantive reforms occurring in the nation's socio-political and educational landscape during the next four years are minimal at best. Unfortunately, many people and organizations will continue to travel along the regressive path of divisiveness, xenophobia, and bigotry in America.

However, educators should not fret because reforms can and must occur at the local and state levels. After all, education in the United States is under state and local control. Many of the reform strategies cited in this book can be implemented under local leadership. The story of C.A. Johnson Preparatory Academy was presented as a testament to the power that a vision, strong leadership, and a passion for children can have in transforming a low-performing urban school to an enterprise for teaching and learning. Many of the reform strategies mentioned were implemented at C.A. Johnson Preparatory Academy from 2002 through 2006.

Local school districts must begin to examine their policies to ensure they promote equal education opportunities for all students. In addition, parents and community stakeholders also must demand that their elected officials are held accountable for their advocacy (or lack thereof) for all children. Should questions or concerns ever arise regarding an elected official's nondiscriminatory advocacy for all children, there is always one attention-getting course of action to address it—the ballot box. A community should move swiftly to remove any school board member who displays any form of bias or discrimination, either implicitly or explicitly, toward any group of children. School boards set policies for children, and as elected officials, they serve at the pleasure of the citizens.

When the Soviet Union launched the first satellite to orbit the Earth 60 years ago, it created an educational revolution in America. The fear of losing the space race propelled Congress to approve the National Defense Education Act, which funded more than a dozen programs meant to help American students compete with the Soviets.

Today, another crisis has emerged. Among the 35 industrialized nations that participate in the international testing initiative known as the Program for International Student Assessment (PISA), the United States now ranks thirty-first in Math. Clearly, America's position as a leader on the world's educational stage is rapidly declining. Unless we begin to implement substantive reforms to meet the needs of our disadvantaged students and children of color, America will not reclaim her rightful position as a world leader in K–12 public and higher education.

I will conclude this book with a thought-provoking quote from G. K. Chesterton: "Education is simply the soul of a society as it passes from one generation to another." The next generation of Americans is looking at us—looking at the soul that we will pass to them. We have examined that soul throughout this book, and we know what needs to be done. Now what?

NOTES

PROLOGUE

The prologue is my personal story, which is etched in my heart and my memory. I leafed through numerous documents such as old school yearbooks, photo albums, school assignments, and other memoirs that sparked recollections of my experiences in both K-12 public and higher education. Conversations with former classmates also served to bring back memories of many experiences and events.

My siblings and I have frequent discussions and reminisce about the "good ole days" when we attended school in Augsburg, Germany; DuPont, Washington; and Columbia, South Carolina. Those discussions and interactions have kept those memories alive and fresh in my mind.

ONE: SEPARATE-AND-UNEQUAL

Tushnet, Mark (1987). *The NAACP's legal strategy against segregated education, 1925-1950*. USA: University of North Carolina Press. This book provides a vivid description and list of Jim Crow laws and makes it clear that their intent was to keep blacks oppressed, uniformed, afraid, and subservient. Many of the laws were directed specifically at black men and forbade them to look at a white woman or even offer to light her cigarette.

Irons, Peter (2004). Jim Crow's Schools Irons' article provides a nice historical perspective and in-depth description of the components of the *Plessy vs. Ferguson* case. The article talks about discriminatory school funding and the extremely low per-pupil allocations for black students in the so-called Black Belt during that time. The article also gives a vivid description of the schools in Dine Hollow, AL, during the Jim Crow era. Retrieved from https://www.aft.org/periodical/american-educator/summer-2004/jim-crows-schools.

Jones, M. (2016, January 30). *Unbelievably Racist World of Classic Children's Literature*. Malcolm Jones's article rekindled memories of the racist books I had read during my years in K-12 public education. Some of those books included stories about the dimwitted George Washington Carver, Little Black Sambo, and the stories that were narrated by Uncle Remus. Other books, such as *Peter Pan* and *Little House on the Prairie*, degraded native Americans. Retrieved from https://www.thedailybeast.com/the-unbelievably-racist-world-of-classic-childrens-literature.

Taylor, J. (1975). *Racial preference and social comparison processes – 36 Years later*. Unpublished master's thesis, University of South Carolina. This is the thesis I wrote for my master's degree. It is essentially a replication of the landmark study that was conducted by Kenneth and Mamie Clark in 1939. My findings were similar to the Clarks'.

The American Black Holocaust Museum's website provided eye-opening pictures and information about Jim Crow and the deplorable conditions in black schools during that era. Retrieved from http://abhmuseum.org/education-for-blacks-in-the-jim-crow-south/

Johnson, H. B. (1998). *Black Wall Street: From Riot to Renaissance in Tulsa's Historic Greenwood District* (Kindle edition). USA: Eakin Press. Prior to writing this book I had never heard of the Black Wall Street. Johnson's book should be a must-read for all Americans! It chronicles how an African American community defied all odds during the early 1900s to build an affluent society that valued education and entrepreneurship.

Gates, H.L. Jr., & Yacovone, D. (2013) *The African Americans: Many Rivers to Cross* (1st ed.). USA: Smiley Books. This textbook provides information on pages 173-182 that I used to compare the ideologies of Booker T. Washington and W.E.B. Du Bois.

TWO: DESEGREGATION DURING THE CIVIL RIGHTS ERA

National Archives (2016). *Brown v. Board of Education Timeline.* This website presents a nice chronological account of the pivotal court cases that led to the *Brown v Board* decision. The cases are listed from *Dred Scott* (blacks could not be citizens of the US) in 1857 to *Brown II* in 1954 (racially segregated public schools are violation of the Equal Protection clause) with a very brief two- or three-sentence summary for each one. Retrieved from https://www.archives.gov/education/lessons/brown-v-board/timeline.html

American Federation of Teachers: A Union of Professionals (2017). This website provides many articles about the history (past and present) of education in America. An article in the Summer of 2004 by Cottrol, Diamond, & Ware entitled *The Legal Strategy That Brought Down 'Separate but Equal' by Toppling School Segregation* highlights the key legal cases that were instrumental in dismantling Jim Crow laws and ideology in America's education system. The article provides key facts and complaints from the five cases that were rolled into the *Brown v. Board*. SC maintained "grossly unequal" schools ($43 per black child; $179 per white child). Louis Redding, a Harvard-educated black lawyer compiled the facts for Delaware's case. Retrieved from https://www.aft.org/periodical/american-educator/summer-2004/naacp-v-jim-crow

Greenwood, M. (2017, February 28). DeVos faces backlash for linking HBCUs to school choice. *The Hill.* In this article, Max Greenwood talks about the outlandish statement Secretary of Education Betsy DeVos made on 2-27-17 calling HBCUs "real pioneers when it comes to school choice." Many people responded by blasting her on twitter, commenting that HBCUs were the only choice to blacks during that time. Several of the tweeters questioned her ability to serve as the secretary of education. The link to the article is retrieved from http://thehill.com/blogs/blog-briefing-room/news/321504-betsy-devos-historically-black-colleges-real-pioneers-on-school

Gates, H.L. Jr., & Yacovone, D. (2013). *The African Americans: Many Rivers to Cross* (1st ed.). USA: Smiley Books. This textbook also provided valuable information about white resistance to desegregation in public and higher education on pages 218-221. Accounts of resistance to integration at Little Rock Central, William Frantz Elementary School (i.e., Ruby Bridges), and the University of Georgia are presented in detail.

Dobbs, C. (2017, July 17). *Desegregation of Higher Education*. This article gives a detailed account of white resistance to allowing black students in institutions of higher education in GA. It gives details of Hamilton Holmes and Charlayne Hunter's attempt to enroll in the University of GA and the Board of Regents' efforts to block their admissions. Violence erupted on campus after they were admitted. Rioters included students and the Ku Klux Klan. Police used tear gas and water hoses to restore order. Retrieved from

http://www.georgiaencyclopedia.org/articles/history-archaeology/desegregation-higher-education

Civil Rights Teaching (2017). *Exploring the History of Freedom Schools*. This website is devoted to providing lessons, resources, and articles about the civil rights movement. The lesson about the freedom schools of the 1960s is informative. It discusses how the Student Nonviolent Coordinating Committee set up the freedom schools in Mississippi during 1964. Nearly 40 schools were established and served nearly 2,500 students, including parents. The organizers of the freedom schools wanted to teach the black children more than the rudimentary "sharecropper" curriculum that was being taught in the schools in Mississippi. Retrieved from https://www.civilrightsteaching.org/voting-rights/exploring-history-freedom-schools/

Sturkey, W. (Summer/Fall 2010). I want to become part of history: Freedom summer, freedom schools, and the freedom news. *Journal of African American History*, vol. 95, No. 3&4, pp. 348-368, Special Issue on Black Print Culture. William Sturkey provides additional information about the freedom schools and the sharecropper education black children received. Once the kids were exposed to a more relevant curriculum that included basic civics and current events, they wanted and demanded a more knowledge.

Davey, H. (2011, February 8). Memoirs in Black and White: Growing up in the Deep South. *Huff Post*. Helen Davey provides an interesting and unique perspective of George Wallace's attempt to block the integration of the University of Alabama. She was present when it happened, and she happens to be white. Davey shares many accounts of racism she witnessed in the Deep South during the 1950s and 1960s. Retrieved from

https://www.huffingtonpost.com/helen-davey/civil-rights-movement_b_816737.html

Dapper Gaming (2011, September 15). *Brown vs. Board of Education Documentary*. [You Tube]. This is a very powerful 9-minute, 59-second video. It gives still photos of the Little Rock Nine, Ruby Bridges, and Linda Brown. The video also discusses *Plessy vs. Ferguson* and the *Brown* decision. While viewing this video, I became aware that Jim Crow was a cartoon-like character who mocked black people. Hence, the racists used this character for the name of their racist laws. Thurgood Marshall was lauded for his brilliance as a lawyer. Retrieved from https://www.youtube.com/watch?v=PLDlqiKXquo

THREE: EQUAL-BUT-UNWANTED IN HIGHER EDUCATION DURING THE AFFIRMATIVE ACTION ERA

Cohen, J., & Solomon, N. (1995, June 26). Clarence Thomas: Poster Boy for Affirmative Action. *The Seattle Times*. This article exposes much of the hypocrisy in Clarence Thomas' anti-affirmative action position. He was raised in poverty in Georgia, and much of his college education was funded via scholarships and financial assistance. Moreover, his admissions into the Yale Law School was based on his race. It seems as if Thomas's position is purely personal. He is driven to prove to the world that he earned everything he accomplished and nothing was given to him. Although he may well have "earned" all of his accolades and accomplishments, the doors to Thomas's success were opened because of one indisputable characteristic – his race. According to the authors, there is an obvious contradiction because "Thomas benefitted enormously from the kind of affirmative-action programs he now seeks to kill." Retrieved from http://community.seattletimes.nwsource.com/archive/?date=19950626&slug=2128294

Messerli, J. (2012, January 7). *Should affirmative action policies, which give preferential treatment based on minority status, be eliminated?* BalancedPolitics.org. The author discusses the pros and cons of affirmative action. Some of the cons are that it: lowers standards, often leads to reverse discrimination, and would lead to a truly color-blind society. Some of the pros are that it: breaks certain stereotypes, promotes diversity, and is needed to compensate for the years of oppression blacks endured. The author seems to have my point of view regarding affirmative action, the program merely opens a door; the person who enters the door must do the hard work. Retrieved by https://www.balancedpolitics.org/affirmative_action.htm

Angyal, C. (2016, June 23). *Affirmative Action is Great for White Women. So Why do they Hate It?* This article appeared in the Huffington Post and focuses on the lawsuit filed by Abigail Fisher against the University of Texas. Unlike the Bakke case, which alleged discrimination on the basis of race, the Fisher case is about discrimination based on gender. Retrieved from https://www.huffingtonpost.com/entry/affirmative-action-white-women_us_56a0ef6ae4b0d8cc1098d3a5

Jacobson, S. (1992, October 8). Manly finally gets a read on education he missed. *Baltimore Sun.* In the article, Jacobson gives a candid account of the exploitation of Dexter Manley. He left Oklahoma State with a second-grade education. While with the Washington Redskins, his teammates knew he could not read. Joe Theismann saw him with a Wall Street Journal one day in the locker room and commented: "Get the funnies, Dexter, you can't read." The article also highlights Dexter's struggles with substance abuse after he left the NFL. Eventually, he learned to read by taking adult classes at a laboratory school and could read his own book – "Educating Dexter" written by Tom Friend. Retrieved from http://articles.baltimoresun.com/1992-10-08/sports/1992282145_1_dexter-reading-the-menu-ottawa-sun

Madamenoire (2011). *14 African American Game Changers that started as Rhodes Scholars.* This online slide show presents bios for 14 blacks who earned the Rhodes Scholarship. They included John Edgar Wideman, Robyn Hadley, Susan Rice, Nnenna Lynch, Cory Booker, Randal Pinkett, Carla Peterman, Rachel Mazyck, Garrett Johnson, Myron Rolle, Ugwechi Amadi, Darryl W. Finkton, Fagan Harris, and Esther Uduechi.

Cory Booker and Susan Rice have prominent in the political arena. Retrieved from http://madamenoire.com/107730/14-african-american-game-changers-that-started-as-rhodes-scholars/

Scott, I. (2017, August 3). *Factors Influencing the Academic Performance of African American Student-Athletes in Historically Black Colleges and Universities.* This article appeared online in the Sport Journal. For his doctoral dissertation, Ian Scott conducted extensive research regarding the impact Prop 48 had on black high school athletes. The new rule "forced" them to study harder, which had a positive long-term effect on their perspective of becoming student-athletes instead of mere jocks. The initial impact was more profound on historically black colleges and universities (HBCUs). He studied student-athletes in 82 HBCUs. One interesting finding was that student-athletes who lived on-campus performed better academically than those who lived off-campus. Retrieved from http://thesportjournal.org/article/factors-influencing-the-academic-performance-of-african-american-student-athletes-in-historically-black-colleges-and-universities/

Temkin, B. (1987, August 14). *Proposition 48 Gives Athletes a Nudge Toward their Books.* This article was online in the Chicago Times. Temkin writes about how Prop 48 positively impacted the mindset of black high school athletes regarding academics. It was a wake-up call to let them know that college sports would not be available to them without at least a 2.0 grade point average and an SAT score of 700. Retrieved from

http://articles.chicagotribune.com/1987-08-14/sports/8703010990_1_recruits-eligibility-richard-lapchick

Zimmer, T. (2014, December 3). *A Look Back at the Higher Education Act.* This is a very informative article about the history of the Higher Education Act (HEA). It gives insightful information about Pell Grants and other financial aid President Johnson authorized in 1965. Although provisions in the HEA made college more affordable, the author states that much more can be done such as streamlining the Free Application for Federal Student Aid, which has a lot of excessive red tape to complete. Retrieved from

https://www.forbes.com/sites/ccap/2014/12/03/a-look-back-at-the-higher-education-act/#32c86fd042e4

Gladieux, L. (1995). Federal Student Aid Policy: A History and an Assessment. The author provides a historical review of federal and financial aid programs that were available through the federal government from 1944 through 1995. In the mid-1990s, loans were by far the largest source of aid, especially for low-income students. Since the mid-1970s, loans have increased from about one-fifth to nearly two-fifths of all student aid. Retrieved from https://www2.ed.gov/offices/OPE/PPI/FinPostSecEd/gladieux.html

Pell Institute's *2013 Report* is a comprehensive 106-page pdf with a wealth of information and historical data about Pell Grants and other financial aid. Retrieved from http://www.pellinstitute.org/downloads/publications-Reflections_on_Pell_June_2013.pdf

Wills, M. (2015, May 18). *James Truslow Adams: Dreaming up the American Dream.* In this article from the JSTOR Daily, Matthew Wills cites the definition of the American Dream that Adams uses in his 1931 book: "A dream of a social order in which each man and each woman shall be able to attain to the fullest stature of which they are innately capable, and be recognized by others for what they are, regardless of the fortuitous circumstances of birth or position." Retrieved from https://daily.jstor.org/james-truslow-adams-dreaming-american-dream/

Quinton, S. (2015, May 5). *The Disproportionate Burden of Student-Loan Debt on Minorities.* The author ttalks about student debt and Elijah Cummings' testimony. Retrieved from https://www.theatlantic.com/education/archive/2015/05/the-disproportionate-burden-of-student-loan-debt-on-minorities/392456/

Jordan, J. (2017, March 1). *From Poverty to Oscar Gold, Viola Davis Shares New Details for Her Incredible Journey: 'I Cannot Believe My Life'.* Viola tells the remarkable story of her rise from poverty in Rhode Island to stardom. I'm still speechless and amazed at the barriers she had to overcome. The photo in this chapter was taken from this article. Retrieved from http://people. om/celebrity/viola-davis-shares-new-details-of-her-journey-poverty-to-oscar-gold/

FOUR: REPORT CARD FOR AMERIC'S EDUCATION SYSTEM DURING THE 20TH CENTURY

Irons, P. (2002). *Jim Crow: The Broken Promise of the Brown Decision.* USA. Penguin Book. This is a very powerful book by Peter Irons, and I used it as resource throughout Part I. Pages 28-38 provided a great description of the dilapidated schools for blacks during the Jim Crow era. The book also provides insight into the mindset many whites harbored in the Deep South regarding the basic curriculum for black children. To many of them, black children only needed to know basic rudimentary skills like tallying and recognizing simple words.

National Trust for Historic Preservation (2017). *Rosenwald Schools.* This website provides links to numerous color photos of the historic Rosenwald Schools as well as links to other information such as the philanthropy of Julius Rosenwald. Because of conversations and site visits with Booker T. Washington of Tuskegee Institute, Rosenwald built state-of-the-art schools for African American children across the South. This effort has been called the most important initiative to advance education for blacks in the early 20th century. By 1928, Rosenwald Schools served one-third of the South's rural black school children and teachers. Between 1917 and 1932, the Rosenwald Foundation constructed 3,357 schools, shops, and teacher homes. Only 10 to 12% remain today. Retrieved from https://savingplaces.org/places/rosenwald-schools#.WdZx7mhSyUn

Pinder, K., & Harrison, E. (2010). *360 Degrees of Segregation: A Historical Perspective of Segregation Era School Equalization Programs in the South United States.* Amsterdam Law Forum, Volume 2, No. 3. In their document, the authors layout the strategies that officials in the Deep South used to thwart desegregation by giving additional funding to black schools to make students more amenable to remaining in their neighborhood schools rather than integrate the white ones. This was the essence of the equalization program. The state of South Carolina was one of the ringleaders of this initiative to thwart desegregation. By 1954, that state's equalization program had built 2,500 new classrooms. Although the new facilities were impressive, education officials noted that the schools stilled lacked necessary instructional materials and supplies. Retrieved from http://amsterdamlawforum.org/article/view/151/300

Zehr, M. A. (2001, August 8). *Schools Grew More Segregated in 1990s.* In her article, Zehr talks about the results of the Harvard Civil Rights Project which indicates that America's schools were "re-segregating" in the 1990s. The study found that 70% of black K-12 students attended predominantly minority schools in the 1998-99 school year, compared with 66% in 1991-92 and 63% in 1980-81. Latinos were even more likely to attend predominantly minority schools; with 76% attending such schools in 1998-99, up from 73% in 1991-92. Retrieved from http://www.edweek.org/ew/articles/2001/08/08/43deseg.h20.html

Edelman, M.W. (2014, July 16). *From Freedom Summer to Freedom Schools.* In this article she wrote for the Huffington Post, Marian Wright Edelman shares a personal perspective of her experience in the Mississippi Freedom Summer Project in 1964. She asserts that the Freedom Schools were designed to keep black children out of harm's way and give them a richer education experience than the sharecropper education the Mississippi public schools offered them. Some volunteers were trained to teach in these "schools," which were held in church basements, on back porches, in parks, and even under trees. She recalled visiting a Freedom School under a tall old oak tree in Greenwood, Mississippi. Edelman is the founder of the Children's Defense Fund (CDF). Edelman's experience in 1964 inspired her to establish two official CDF Freedom Schools in 1995 with a rigorous curriculum to develop scholars. One was in South Carolina and the other in Missouri. Retrieved from

http://www.childrensdefense.org/programs/freedomschools/?referrer=https://www.google.com/

History.com (2017). *The Space Race.* This website provides a very informative article about Russia's launching of Sputnik (Russian word for "traveler") and the frenzy that led to the race for space between Russia and the United States. The launch occurred on 10-4-1957 and marked the beginning of the cold war. The website has colorful pictures of Sputnik, cosmonauts, and Laika (the little Russian dog that was the first animal launched into space). Retrieved from http://www.history.com/topics/space-race

Bartels, M. (2017, August 22). *The unbelievable life of a forgotten genius who turned Americans' space dreams into reality.* Meghan Bartels' article was published in Business Insider. She writes about the life and accomplishments of Katherine Johnson. Many of NASA's first missions were made possible by Johnson's calculations. She was considered a human computer. Bartels also commented on the movie *Hidden Figures,* in which Taraji P. Henson portrayed Johnson. I saw the movie and it captured the "separate but equal" society that existed in NASA at that time. Even though everyone was on the same team trying to win the race-for-space against Russia, it seemed as if racism or keeping the blacks "in their place" was more important to many workers at NASA. Retrieved from http://www.history.com/topics/space-race

National Assessment of Educational Progress (2017). This NAEP website is the largest nationally representative and continuing assessment of what America's students know and can do in various subject areas. It has a plethora of historical data regarding the nation's report card and the achievement gap between black and white students. Between 1971 and 1994, the reading gap between black and white 17-year-olds has narrowed by 40%. The math gap has also narrowed during that period but not as much. The average NAEP science scores for the nation increased 4 points between 2009 and 2015 in both grades 4 and 8, but did not change significantly at grade 12. Scores for most student groups at grades 4 and 8 were higher in 2015 compared to 2009, but were not significantly different at grade 12. At grades 4 and 8, Black and Hispanic students made greater gains than White students, causing the achievement gap to narrow in comparison to 2009. Retrieved from https://nces.ed.gov/nationsreportcard/

FIVE: CURRENT CHALLENGES IN PUBLIC EDUCATION

National Center for Education Statistics (2017). *Racial/Ethnic Enrollment in Public Schools*. This website provides a wealth of demographic data for students and teachers in K-12 public education. In the fall of 2014, the percentage of students enrolled in public elementary and secondary schools who were white was less than 50 percent (49.5 percent) for the first time and represents a decrease from 58 percent in fall 2004. In contrast, the percentage who were Hispanic increased from 19 to 25 percent during the same period. I made frequent "visits" to this site. Retrieved from https://nces.ed.gov/programs/coe/indicator_cge.asp

U.S. Department of Education (2016). *The State of Racial Diversity in the Educator Workforce*. This 42-page report is presented in the form of a pdf and can be downloaded. A treasure chest of data is presented in 27 different figures and charts. The K-12 public education workforce is overwhelmingly homogenous (82 percent white). Over time, educator diversity has increased. In the 1987–88 school year, 13 percent of public school teachers were teachers of color compared to 18 percent in the 2011–12 school year. While the proportion of all teachers of color has increased over time, this trend is not the result of increases in the proportion of teachers in all non-white racial and ethnic categories. For example, the proportion of teachers who were black decreased slightly over this period. Two percent of individuals who are preparing to be teachers are enrolled at HBCUs, but 16 percent of all black teacher candidates attend HBCUs. Education leaders are also predominantly white. In the 2011–12 school year, only 20 percent of public school principals were individuals of color.

Retrieved from https://www2.ed.gov/rschstat/eval/highered/racial-diversity/state-racial-diversity-workforce.pdf

Rosenthal, R., &. Jacobson, L. (1963). Teachers' expectancies: Determinants of pupils' IQ gains. *Psychological Reports, 19,* 115-118. The results of this classic study continue to ring true in education today. Simply stated, students rise or fall to the expectations of their teachers. Students believed to be on the verge of great academic success performed in accordance with these expectations; students not labeled this way did not. Later research has supported Rosenthal's original conclusion that teacher expectations can have a substantial effect on students' scholastic performance. This can be problematic even today, especially when teachers have opinions and stereotypes related to having low expectations for black children.

Taylor, Wandy W. (2017, April) [personal conversations]. Through both formal and informal conversations, Dr. Wandy W. Taylor provided valuable insights about multiculturalism, cultural competence, and culturally responsive pedagogy. She shared incidents that occurred during her time as the principal of a high-diverse, high-poverty elementary school in Lilburn, GA. One incident involved a time when a white teacher asked her third-graders to write about the items in their garage. Most of the students came from low-income families and their homes (i.e., mostly apartments or hotel rooms) did not have a garage. She also shared about the time a teacher mistakenly called an Asian parent an "Oriental." This was due to a lack of cultural competence and awareness. Dr. Taylor is now an education consultant with Taylor & Taylor Education Consultants. Wandy@tandteducationconsltants.com

Sanders, W. (2016, October 19). *Racial Equity: 2,000 Seattle Teachers to Wear BLM Shirts to Class.* Some 2,000 teachers staged a rally after on-line threats were received by one of the district's elementary schools over a black community outreach program that was held earlier. About 2,000 teachers assembled on the campus of Garfield High School in Seattle clad in Black Lives Matter T-shirts. The teachers staged the demonstration in a quest for racial equity. This show of solidarity served to bond the Garfield students with their teachers. They respected the fact that the teachers supported them. Retrieved from https://blackmattersus.com/18354-racial-equity-2000-seattle-teachers-to-wear-blm-shirts-to-class/

Mettler K. (2016, September 2). *A Texas teacher named her class the j-word. Her racial slur defense: ignorance.* Bell Manor Elementary School is in a town between Fort Worth and Dallas. The teacher intended to create togetherness in the classroom through a team-building exercise. Teams were given nicknames. One group of children claimed the name "Dream Team." Another got "Jighaboos." When one student's father found out, he was appalled and contacted the local media. The teacher, Kristi Chapel, claimed she did not know the word was a racial slur. A clear example of cultural incompetence. This is yet another example of the need for teachers to receive training and professional development in multicultural education. Retrieved from https://www.washingtonpost.com/news/morning-mix/wp/2016/09/02/a-texas-teacher-named-her-class-the-j-word-her-racial-slur-defense-ignorance/?utm_term=.eeaba06a3011

U.S. Department Education (2014). *Expansive Survey of America's Public Schools Reveals Troubling Racial Disparities.* U. S. Secretary of Education Arne Duncan says America still does not provide equal education for all students, especially for African Americans. He cited disparities in discipline and access to highly-qualified teaches. Secretary Duncan's comments provide a good segue for a discussion of the "criminalization" of black students and their pathway to the infamous school-to-prison pipeline. Retrieved from https://www.ed.gov/news/press-releases/expansive-survey-americas-public-schools-reveals-troubling-racial-disparities

Shropshire, T. (2012, April 17). *Police handcuff, arrest 6-year-old black girl at Georgia school.* Six-year-old Salencia Johnson was arrested, handcuffed, and taken to the local police station after she had a temper tantrum at Creekside Elementary School in Milledgeville, GA. The girl's aunt, Candace Ruff, went with the child's mother to pick her up from the police station. She said Salencia had been in a holding cell and complained about the handcuffs being too tight. There are many problems with this incident: (a) the principal never should have called the police, (b) kids having a tantrum need time to deescalate, and (c) the kid still received a long-term suspension. Retrieved from https://rollingout.com/2012/04/17/police-handcuff-arrest-6-year-old-black-girl-at-georgia-school/

Pollock, H. (2016, May 24). *A middle school student was arrested for 'stealing' free milk from his cafeteria.* On 5-10-16, at Graham Park Middle School in Triangle, VA, Ryan Turk went to the lunch line and grabbed a carton of milk. Since he was on the school's free lunch program, he was supposed to be able the get a 65-cent carton of milk free. But a school resource officer (SRO) was on-site and accused him of stealing the milk. An argument ensued when Ryan tried to pull away from the officer. He was handcuffed, arrested, and charged with larceny. Moreover, he was suspended for theft, being disrespectful, and using a cell phone in school. Sadly, the student had to appear in court, which placed him in the school-to-prison pipeline. Once again, an SRO was involved in a school discipline issue with a black student that should have been handled by the principal. Retrieved from https://munchies.vice.com/en_us/article/pgvv47/a-middle-school-student-was-arrested-for-stealing-free-milk-from-his-cafeteria

National Center for Education Statistic's (2015). *Public School Safety and Discipline: 2013-14.* This 55-page report contains numerous charts, tables, graphs, and data about school-based policing. According to the report, 43% of all U.S. public schools – including 63% of middle schools and 64% of high schools – employed school resource officers (SROs) during the 2013-2014 school year. More than 46,000 full-time and 36,000 part-time officers were on duty during that time, and the numbers are expected to increase. Middle and high schools have utilized SROs for years, and now a growing number of elementary schools are joining them. More than 73% of school with 1,000 or more students have SROs. Retrieved from

http://www.tssbulletproof.com/school-resource-officers-fastest-growing-area-law-enforcement/

Farner, K. (2017, June 19). *School board hears report, recommendations from discipline committee.* This news article appeared in the Gwinnett Daily Post. One of the nation's largest and most diverse school systems has made a huge mistake by making some of their rules more "subjective" to interpretation. So-called "disrespectful conduct" is now a major rule violation. As always, acts of disrespect are subject to cultural interpretations and those interpretations can be influenced by preexisting biases. Retrieved from http://www.gwinnettdailypost.com/local/school-board-hears-report-recommendations-from-discipline-committee/article_73ceb23f-c2bb-5b03-b6fa-15793d94c9f0.html

Botelho, G. (2012, May 23). *What Happened the Night Trayvon Martin died?* The Trayvon Martin story has been well-chronicled. It speaks to the stereotypes that continue to perpetuate low expectations for young blacks, especially in public school. Trayvon was killed simply because he was a young black boy wearing a hoodie. Retrieved from

http://www.cnn.com/2012/05/18/justice/florida-teen-shooting-details/index.html

Geraldo Rivera, a man of color, commented on *Fox and Friends* on March 23, 2012, that "I think the hoodie is as much responsible for Trayvon Martin's death as George Zimmerman was." This created outrage in the black community and launched a Million Hoodie March in New York City in memory of Trayvon. Retrieved from

http://www.foxnews.com/politics/2012/03/23/trayvon-martins-hoodie-and-george-zimmerman-share-blame.html

Schott Report (2015*). Black Lives Matter: The Schott 50 State Report on Public Education and Black Males.* This 68-page report can be accessed on-line. Black males continue to be suspended from school at an alarming rate. The national graduation rate for black males is 59% compared to 80% for white males. This comprehensive report contains discipline and graduation data for all 50 states. The data in tables five and six were taken from page 25 in the report. New York City Schools has the largest number of black males enrolled (143,972); however, they only have a 28% graduation rate. Retrieved from http://www.blackboysreport.org/2015-black-boys-report.pdf

SIX: CURRENT CHALLENGES IN HIGHER EDUCATION

Preston, D. C. (2017). *Untold Barriers for Black Students in Higher Education: Placing Race at the Center of Developmental Education*. Atlanta, GA. Southern Education Foundation. This 40-page document provides a massive amount of data regarding HBCUs and their struggles. The section on developmental education (DE) was especially enlightening and informative. Statistics show that more than half of all first-time students enroll in DE at two-year colleges. At two-year institutions, more than 70 percent of black students enroll in at least one DE course. At four-year institutions, black students are almost twice as likely to enroll in DE than all students combined. Also, Black students are more likely to need DE courses in both Math and English. In comparison to other ethnic groups, and even Pell-eligible students, black students are more likely to be required to complete DE at both the two- and four-year institutions. Retrieved from file:///C:/Users/jim/Documents/BOOK/Untold-Barriers-for-Black-Students-in-Higher-ED.pdf

Stewart, P. (2014, May 29). N.C. *Legislators Target Elizabeth City State*. In this article, Pearl Stewart reported that the North Carolina State Senate wants to close Elizabeth City State, a historically black university, because it is "small and unprofitable." This speaks to the plight that many HBCUs are facing; namely, threats of defunding and dramatic declines in enrollment. Morris Brown College in Atlanta faced a similar threat of closing in 2009 when its enrollment plummeted to a mere 44 students. Retrieved from

http://diverseeducation.com/article/64580/

Atlanta Public Schools TV (2014, September 11). *First Lady of the United States, Michelle Obama, speaking at Booker T. Washington High School*. [You Tube].

In this nearly 26-minute video on YouTube, First Lady Michelle Obama speaks to students at high-poverty Booker T. Washington High School in Atlanta to kick-off her "Reaching Higher" campaign. She talks about the importance of education and going to college to escape poverty. She said "rich kids all over the county know this stuff. You need to know it, too." Mrs. Obama displayed an uncanny ability to connect with people. Retrieved from https://www.youtube.com/watch?v=uaJV99C7VVw

Noel, M. (2016). *ROI on HBCUs: The Role of Historically Black Colleges in the 21st Century.* Noel talks about how HBCUs created the black middle class in America. They produced 40% of black members of congress and 50% of black lawyers and judges. The article also speaks about the number of black Pell Grant recipients (70%) and Prince Adubu, a Morehouse senior who was eligible for a Rhodes Scholarship. Retrieved from https://www.forbes.com/sites/under30network/2016/05/02/roi-on-hbcus-the-role-of-historically-black-colleges-in-the-21st-century/#55fc72b8720b

The American Association of State Colleges and Universities (January 2017). *The Top Ten Higher Education State Policy Issues for 2017.* This Policy Matters Brief outlines the key challenges that institutions of higher education must face. They include: Funding, Affordability, Building a Skilled Workforce, Undocumented and DACA Students, Campus Sexual Assaults, Guns on Campus, Institutional Productivity and Student Success, Academic Freedom, Student Debt Management, and Dual Enrollment. Retrieved from

http://www.aascu.org/policy/publications/policy-matters/Top10Issues2017.pdf

SEVEN: HIGHER EDCUATION – REFORM ACTIONS NEEDED

The American Association of State Colleges and Universities (2016). *Preparing Teachers in Today's Challenging Context: Key Issues, Policy Directions, and Implications for Leaders of AASCU Universities.* This 48-page document provides a comprehensive overview of the challenges that exist in many of our nation's institutions of higher education. A lot of the challenges are in the areas of teacher preparation and training, especially because of the ever-increasing diversity in K-12 public education. Many of the changes must occur through policies, procedures, and articulation agreements. Retrieved from https://www.aascu.org/ AcademicAffairs/TeacherEdReport.pdf

Tepper, T. (2016, September 29). *One Way Crushing Student Loan Debt Has Helped Millennial Parents.* This article appeared in Money Magazine and Taylor Tepper talks about how student loans are crushing both parents and graduates. The author writes about the little-known 529 Plans and how they can be used on the front-end to help minimize the overwhelming debt that can fall on families after graduation. Retrieved from http://time.com/money/4511356/millennial-parents-college-costs/

National Student Campaign Against Hunger & Homelessness (2016). *Report: Hunger on Campus.* The executive summary of the report is on this website with a link to the pdf of the complete report, which can be downloaded. The report involved a survey of 3,765 students in 12 states. Sixty-four percent of the students with food insecurity also had some type of housing insecurity; 57% of the black students reported some sort of food insecurity. Student poverty is a major problem on many college campuses. Problems with food or housing harm students' educational efforts. Of the food insecure students in the study, 32 percent believed that hunger or housing problems had an impact on their education.

Retrieved from https://studentsagainsthunger.org/hunger-on-campus/

Jacobs, J. (2012, March 9). *Some Teens Start College Work Early via Dual Enrollment.* My knowledge of dual enrollment classes extends back to my years as a high school principal. The students at my school took courses at local college for dual credit. This is a nice article that served as a "refresher" for me. As an advocate for dual enrollment, I agree that dual courses expose students to rigorous classes that prepare them for college success, builds their confidence, and speeds their way to an affordable degree. There is growing evidence to indicate that students who take dual credit course do better in college. Retrieved from https://www.usnews.com/education/best-colleges/articles/2012/03/09/some-teens-start-college-work-early-via-dual-enrollment

EIGHT: PUBLIC EDUCATION – REFORM ACTIONS NEEDED

Will, M. (2016, May 10). *Still Another Survey, Teachers are Feeling Stressed, Discounted.* An online survey of 3,328 teachers indicated that most of them feel under-respected, under-paid, under-appreciated, and over-worked. Retrieved from

http://www.edweek.org/ew/articles/2016/05/11/still-another-survey-says-teachers-are-feeling.html

Walker, T. (2016, May 19). *Snapshot of the Teaching Profession: What's Changed over a Decade?* Walker lists five major changes that are happening in public education: (1) the teaching profession is still predominantly white at about 83%; (2) the profession is getting greener with 12% having less than four years of experience; (3) teachers spend a lot of time in the classroom; (4) teachers' attitude have remained consistent for the past decade; and (5) teachers appear to accept the notion that poverty is a factor. The student-teacher racial gap is real (the pie chart in the book was taken from this article). Retrieved from http://neatoday.org/2016/05/19/snapshot-of-the-teaching-profession/

Avila, J., & Hobbs, T. (2017, September 6). *Teacher Shortage Prompts Some States to Lower the Bar.* Wall Street Journal. In the face of a worsening teacher shortage, several states (e.g., MN, AZ, & IL) around the country are loosening their requirements for credentials that will make it easier to teach in public school classrooms.

Center for Public Education (2016). *Fixing the Holes in the Teacher Pipeline: An Overview of Teacher Shortages.* Barth, Dillon, Hull, & Higgins wrote this comprehensive 36-page white paper. It provides an abundance of information about teacher preparation, training, and recruitment programs to address teacher shortages. Retrieved from http://www.centerforpubliceducation.org/Main-

Menu/Staffingstudents/An-Overview-of-Teacher-Shortages-At-a-Glance/Overview-of-Teacher-Shortages-Full-Report-PDF.pdf

Kamenetz, A. (2017, April 10). *Having just one black teacher can keep black kids in school*. The title of the article is self-explanatory with implications for public education. Retrieved from http://www.npr.org/sections/ed/2017/04/10/522909090/having-just-one-black-teacher-can-keep-black-kids-in-school

NINE: C. A. JOHNSON PREPARATORY ACADEMY: REVIVING AN ALL-BLACK URBAN HIGH SCHOOL

My personal portfolio for C.A. Johnson Preparatory Academy, which was compiled during the period from 2001- 2006, served as the primary reference for this chapter. The portfolio contains a copy of the comprehensive report that was compiled by the seven-member task force; the Power Point presentation that was delivered to the Board of School Commissioners for approval; and the signed contract between Richland School District One and Benedict College. The portfolio also contained my contemporaneous notes of conversations, formal classroom observations, action plans, and various other documents and memorabilia.

Taylor, J. (September 2017). I had conversations with Rachell Wallace, Terri McClain-Hill, Brittany Payne-Bruce, Chad Washington to determine the whereabouts of key graduates of the C. A. Johnson Preparatory Class of 2006. Many of the graduates are successful. Maurice Lindsay has published a book; Katherine and Amber are attorneys; Chad is an athletics director; LaKesa has her master's and is working in corporate America; Stephanie is a captain in the military; Bouttry is a police officer; and Raheem earned an associate's degree.

TEN: CONCLUSION

This chapter was written primarily as a compilation of the preceding chapters. The incidents that involved Congressman Scalise and Charlottesville were current events that dominated the news media during the summer of 2017.

Cherng, H. (2017, September 26). *Teachers report weaker relationships with students of color, children of immigrants.* Science Daily. Cherng concludes that the poor teacher-student relations can be addressed through teacher training in cultural awareness. Retrieved from https://www.sciencedaily.com/releases/2017/09/170926105439.htm

Barshay, J. (2016, December 6) The Hechinger Report. US now ranks near the bottom among 35 industrialized nations in math on the Program for International Student Assessment (PISA). This test is administered every three years and marks the second straight time (2012 and 2015) scores for US student have declined. Retrieved from http://hechingerreport.org/u-s-now-ranks-near-bottom-among-35-industrialized-nations-math/

I personally developed the four-step model to illustrate how the book has taken us through the first two steps (Inspect and Select). Plans for reform must be developed before America's education system can move into the third step.

Table		Page
1.	Black Student Enrollment (Medical and Law School 1978 to 1988)	29
2.	Pell Recipients by Race 2013	38
3.	Scoring Rubric for America's Performance with Public Education for Black Students	57
4.	Percentages of Title I and non-Title I Students Scoring Proficient Reading on State Grade 4 Reading Tests	70
5.	Highest Ranked Districts for Black Male Graduates	81
6.	Lowest Ranked Districts for Black Male Graduates	83
7.	Percentage of Students in Developmental Education Classes by Family Income	92
8.	Completion of Gateway Courses for African American Students at Two-Year and Four-Year Institutions	95
9.	Percentage of Pell Grant Recipients at HBCUs	101
10.	Race and Student Debt	103
11.	Institutions Receiving the Most Funding from the Federal Government in 2016	111
12.	Adjusted Cohort Graduation Rates (Percentages) for Class of 2012	135
13.	Teacher-Student Racial Gap	139
14.	Action Plan #1: School Climate	168
15.	Action Plan #2: Curriculum	170
16.	Action Plan #3: Instruction	172
17.	Action Plan #4: Community and Parent Relations	174
18.	Exit Exams (First Attempt) Top Gains Among South Carolina's High Schools 2003	177
19.	SAT Scores for South Carolina High Schools 2005	179

Figures	Page
1. Four-Step Process for Reform	186
2. Four-Step Process for Reform (Steps Completed)	188

Index

A

Abecedarian Project, 133
Academic freedom, 113-115
   in higher education, 113, 114
   right-vs-left conflict, 114
   "Sex Week", 114
Advanced Placement courses, 77, 78
Adventures of Huckleberry Finn (Twain), 6
Affirmative action, 26-31, 41, 42
Alexander, Sen. Lamar, 116
Alexander, Michelle, 62
   "invisible racism" in America, 62
   The New Jim Crow: Mass Incarceration in the
   age of Colorblindness, 62
Amendments to Constitution, 3
   13th, 14th, 15th, 3
American College Test, 33
American Council on Education, 8, 45
   Investigation of black schools, 8, 45
American Dream, 42, 43, 59, 62, 77, 88, 102, 104, 105, 107, 112,
   pathway to, 77, 88
Annie E. Casey Foundation ,69
Ashley, Maurice, 185
Augsburg, Germany, v

B

Bakke, Allan, 27
Banks, James, 56
Barnett, Gov. Ross, 22
Bell Manor ES, 64, 65
   cultural incompetence, 64
   "Jighaboos", 64, 65
Benson, Thomasenia, 157, 159- 161
Black Belt, 8, 10, 12
Black enrollment in law & medical school, 29
Black Lives Matter, 65, 66, 115
   solidarity among teachers in Seattle, 65
   support for diversity, 66
   University of Missouri, 115
Black Thursday, 2
Black, Trexton, 159
Black Wall Street, 10, 11
   black businesses, 10
   Greenwood District, 10
   mob violence, 11
Boiling v. Sharpe (1950), 16
Bolden, Gen. Charles, Jr., 146, 154
Booker, Cory, 34
Bootie, Judge William, 21, 22
   orders the integration of UGA, 22
Bouttry, Demetrius, 180
Bridges, Abron & Lucille, 18
Bridges, Ruby, 18-20, 24
Briggs v. Elliott (1950), 16

Brookings Institution, 103

Brown, J. Anthony, 154

Brown v. Board of Education (1950), 15-18, 21, 22, 25, 47, 52

    racially segregated public schools are unconstitutional, 15, 16

C

C. A. Johnson HS, 31, 32, 154, 155, 181

    task force to create a "renaissance", 155

C.A. Johnson Preparatory Academy (CAJPA), 154-182, 190

    academic achievement, 176-180

    Action Plan #1 (Climate), 168

    Action Plan #2 (Curriculum), 170, 171

    Action Plan # 3 (Instruction), 172, 173

    Action Plan #4 (Community), 174

    Atmosphere, Academics, & Attitude 181, 182

    exit exam scores, 177, 178

    guiding principles, 166, 167

    partnership with Benedict College, 155, 156, 171

    SAT scores, 179

"CAJ Ten", 32

Carver ES, v

Catapult Learning, Inc., 136, 137

Census Bureau, 66, 68

Center for Public Education, 133

Center on Education Policy, 69, 71, 147

    Title I vs. non-Title I students, 69

Charlottesville, VA, 187

    neo-Nazi protest, 187

Cherng, Hua-Yu, 189

    importance of teacher-student relationships, 189

    relapse of education for unwanted children, 189

Chesterton, G. K., 191

Children's Defense Fund, 51, 67

    schools, 51

    transformative curriculum, 51

Civil Rights Act of 1964, 25, 57

Civil Rights Era, 14, 24, 45, 102

Clark & Clark Doll Study, 6, 7, 12, 16

    low self-esteem, 6, 12

    stereotypes, 7, 12

Classroom instruction, 50, 171-173

Coahoma Community College, 99

Cognitive dissonance, 28

Coleman Report, 53, 54

    achievement gap, 53

    busing-for-desegregation, 53

    racial and economic divide, 53

    standardized testing, 53

    teachers matter, 54

College professors, 120-121

    lack of teaching skills, 121

    "publish or perish", 121

Community Colleges, 89-90

    decline in enrollment, 90

    enrollment by ethnicity, 90

    graduation rates, 90

Community relations, 174, 175

Conceal-carry of handguns, 118

Creekside, ES, 73
   ambiguous school policy, 73
   six-year-old arrested, 73

Cruz, Julio, vi

Culture competence, 64, 65

Culturally responsive pedagogy (CRP), 56, 172

Culturally responsive teaching (CRT), 139

Cummings, Rep. Elijah, 37

Cunningham, Bobby, 180

Curriculum, 7-9, 48-51, 57
   adaptive, 49, 50
   during segregation, 7, 9
   "sharecropper education", 49, 51
   situational, 49
   taught, 49
   written, 48

D

Davis v. Prince Edward County, 16

Davis, Viola, 40, 41, 43
   Central Falls HS, 41
   Julliard School of Drama, 41
   Triple Crown of Acting, 41

Dawes, Dominique, 34

De facto discrimination, viii, 188

De jure racism, 4, 62

Desegregation, 17, 18, 23

Developmental Education, 91-95, 106
   for African American students, 91
   completion rates, 94, 95
   lack of quality teachers, 95
   low income students, 92, 93
   "unwanted-but-necessary-evil", 92
   Ohio data 92, 93
   remedial courses, 91

De Vos, Betsy, 20, 110, 189
   "HBCUs schools of choice", 20
   spread of charter schools, 189

Dine Hollow School, 8, 9

Disengaged students, 56, 79

Diversity gap, 55

Dual enrollment classes, 122, 156

Du Bois, W.E.B., 11-13

Duncan, Arne, 72

E

Edelman, Marian W., 51

Educating Dexter (Tom Friend), 35, 36

Eisenhower, President Dwight D., 24

Elizabeth City State University, 98
   "small and unprofitable", 98

Engaged students, 50, 56, 79, 156

Enhancement Program, 156

Epic of America (James T. Adams), 26

Epps, Dr. Ronald, 118, 155-157
   concerns regarding CAJ, 155
   "egregious in education", 118
   superintendent of Richland One, 155

Equal-but-unwanted, v, viii, 25, 26, 28, 188, 189

Equalized school funding, 47, 48

Equal Protection Clause, 16
Every Student Succeeds Act (ESSA), 140
Eye dialect, 4

F
Facility walk-through, 159, 160
FAIR policies in higher education, 107
    Funding, 110-113
    Affordable, 116, 122
    Instructors, 120-122
    Relevant, 124
Faubus, Gov. Orval ,17
Federal marshals, 18, 19
Financial Aid Programs, 25, 36-38
Fisher, Abigail, 31
    affirmative action lawsuit, 31
    alleged discrimination based on her race, 31
Ford, Vince, 156
Four-Step Model for Reform, 185-189
    inspection-selection-preparation-implementation, 185-189
Freedman's Bureau, 25
Freedom schools, 49-51

G
Gang activity at CAJPA, 164, 167, 169
    Bloods and Folks, 164, 169
    gang leaders supporting the principal, 169
Gebhart v. Ethel (1950), 16
George, Eddie, 34
George Washington Rabbit, 5

Georgia General Assembly, 21
    discriminatory admissions laws 21
Glenn, John, 52
"Good teaching matters", 95, 152
Good to Great (Collins), 82
Goss v. Lopez (1975), 131
Grad-Nation, 134, 135
    effects of absences, 134
    effects of poverty, 134
    graduation gaps for states, 135
Great Depression, 2
Gurley, O.W., 10
Gwinnett County Public Schools, 74, 75
    disproportionate suspensions, 74
    subjective interpretation of rules, 74, 75
    teacher-student culture gap, 74

H
H-1-B visas, 161
Hard work, 37-40, 43
Harris, Joel Chandler, 4
Harvard University, 11, 27
Harvard Civil Rights Project, 48
    de facto segregation, 48
    "re-segregation", 48
    "white flight", 48
Heatley, James, 162
Hendrix, Amber, 180
Henry, Barbara, 19, 20
Henson, Taraji, P., 52
Hidden Figures, 52

Higher Education, 77, 78, 88, 89, 106-108, 110, 111, 118, 119, 120, 120-124

    admissions policies, 77, 78, 89

    antiquated model, 124

    competency-based model, 124

    curriculum reform, 124

    diploma factories, 124

    enrollment of African Americans, 89

    funding, 110, 111

    safe environments, 118, 119

Higher Education Act of 1965, 37

Hilton, William, 161, 164

Historically Black Colleges & Universities (HBCUs), 20, 21, 32, 39, 96-101, 106, 107, 112, 113, 180

    created the black middle class, 100

    enrollment, 96

    graduation rates, 96, 97, 99

    number in the US, 96

    percentage of Pell Grant recipients, 101

    problems with underfunding, 97, 98

    serving low-income students, 99

Hitler, Adolph, 185

Holmes, Hamilton, 21, 22

Hood, James A., 23

Hopkins, Dr. Ronnie, 155

Howard University, 31, 39, 46, 97, 98, 99

Hunger on Campus Report, 119, 120

    food insecurity, 119

    poverty rates for college students, 119

    some innovative programs, 120

Hunter, Charlayne, 21, 22

I

Informal observations, 163-165

    operations, 163

    student & teachers, 165

J

Jackson State College, 22

Jemison, Dr. Mae, 185

Jensen, Arthur, 54

    IQ scores for African Americans, 54

    eugenics point of view, 54

Jim Crow Era, 2-13, 24, 44, 54, 72, 184

    culture, 2, 3, 24, 54

    oppressive laws, 3, 44, 72, 184

    racial segregation, 3, 4

    school funding, 7, 8

    segregated schools, 4

    separate facilities, 8, 9, 45

    substandard schools, 7, 9

Johns Hopkins Report, 84

    impact of having one black teacher, 84

Johnson, Katherine, 52, 53

    human computer, 52, 53

    math genius, 52, 53

    NASA, 52, 53

Johnson, President Lyndon, 25, 26, 36, 67, 132, 185

    War on Poverty, 36, 67

Jones, Stephanie, 180

K

K-12 Public Education, 85, 86, 125-153
  components of a discipline code, 129-131
  culture gap, 86, 137-140
  graduation rates, 134, 135
  impact of poverty on children, 132
  policy and governance, 126-128
  pre-kindergarten, 133
  reform action needed, 131, 133, 134, 137, 140, 145
  school readiness, 132-133
  zero tolerance policies, 126

Kennedy, President John F., 23, 24, 185
Kennedy, Robert F., 22
King, Jr. Dr. Martin L., 14, 72, 99
Ku Klux Klan, 11, 114, 187

L

Ladson-Billings, Gloria, 56
Laughbon High School, vi
LGBTQ, 100, 115
Lindsay, Maurice, 180
Little Rock's Central HS, 17
Little Rock Nine, 24
Lomax, Michael, 113
  United Negro College Fund, 113
Look Magazine, 19
Low expectations, 86

M

Malone, Vivian, 23
Manley, Dexter, 34-36, 39
  illiterate in college 34

Marshall, Thurgood, 14, 15, 72, 99
Martin, Trayvon, 78, 79
McClinton, Isaac, 180
McGraw, LaKesa, 180
McLaurin v. Oklahoma (1950), 15, 21
Meredith, James, 21, 24
Morehouse College, 99, 100
Morris Brown College, 98
  problems with funding and accreditation, 98
Mouton, Nikki, 172
Multiculturalism, 63-66
  multicultural education, 65
  schools becoming more diverse, 63, 66
Myers, Katherine, 180

N

NAACP, 12, 14, 15, 21, 22, 45
  Legal Defense & Education Fund, 14, 15
National Aeronautics and Space Administration (NASA), 52
National Assessment Educational Progress (NAEP), 54
National Center for Education Statistics, 63, 74
National Collegiate Athletic Association (NCAA), 33, 43
National Comprehensive Center for Teachers, 66
  "need for multicultural education", 66
National Dropout Prevention Center, 136

National Student Clearinghouse Research Center, 90

    decline in community college enrollment, 90

Nation's Report Card, 54

Neo-Nazis, 114, 187

No Child Left Behind Act, 140

O

Obama, Barack, 78, 89, 98, 143, 185

    American College Promise program, 89

    Excellent Educators for All initiative, 143, 145

    Harvard Law Review, 185

Obama, Michelle, 102, 105

    speaking at a high school in Atlanta, 102

Ogubu, John U., 56

O'Neal, Shaquille "Shaq", 40

Oppression, 44

Oprah Winfrey Show, 20

P

Paine, Steven, 146

Park MS, 73

    65-cent carton of milk, 73

    SRO arrests student, 73

Patillo, Melba, 17

Pell Grant, 37, 38, 43, 110

Pell Grant Institute Report, 38

Pence, Mike, 189

Perry, Tyler, 43

Pew Research Center, 146

Pledge of Allegiance, 23

Policymakers, 13, 114, 115, 117

Post-racial society, 97, 98

Poverty, 36, 67-71, 119, 120, 132, 152

    after college, 123

    characteristics, 67

    official poverty rates, 68

Powell, Colin, 41

Prescriptive Educational Plan, 169

Prestigious institutions, 27, 97

    increase in black student enrollment, 27

    graduation rates for African Americans, 97

Prince Edward School District, 16, 18

Pringle, Mickey, 180

Program for International Student Assessment (PISA), 146, 147, 153, 191

    "lack of respect for teachers", 146

    2015 test results, 146

    US students continue to lag behind, 153

Proposition 48, 26, 33-36, 42, 43

    impact on HBCUs, 33, 34

    reaction in the black community, 43

    revised eligibility requirements, 33

R

Racial discrimination, 44, 59, 184

Racism, 2, 22, 24, 62, 65

Racist school literature, 4-6

Reconstruction Era, 25

Regents of the University of California v Bakke (1978), 27, 28,

Affirmative Action is constitutional, 27

racial quotas are unconstitutional, 27

"reverse discrimination", 27, 30, 42

Report Card, 57-59

  achievement, 58

  America's education system, 57

  curriculum, 58

  facilities, 57

  scoring rubric, 57

  teacher effectiveness, 58

Reuben, Earl, vii, 32

Review of school data, 158

Rhodes Scholars (African American), 34, 39, 40

  Carla Peterman, 39

  Cory Booker, 34

  John Wideman, 39, 40

  Myron Rolle, 39, 40

  Nnenna Lynch, 34

Rice, Condoleezza, 185

Rivera, Geraldo, 79

  Fox and Friends, 79

  "you dress like a thug", 79

Rivers, Dr. Thomas, 161, 180

Roark, Dale, 34-36

Robinson, David, 34

Roosevelt, Franklin D., 2

Rosenwald, Julius, 45, 46

  donations to HBCU's, 46

Rosenwald Schools, 46, 47

Rowland, Dick, 10

S

Sanders, Sen. Bernie, 116, 117

  "free tuition", 116, 117

SAT, 26, 32, 33, 43

Scalise, Sen. Steve, 187

School boards, 126-131, 190

School climate, 167-169, 181

School facilities, 45-48, 57

School policies, 72-78, 126-131

  biased, 72, 73

  discipline, 72, 126-131

  zero tolerance, 128

School resource officers (SROs), 73-75, 131

  GA Juvenile Justice Reform Bill, 131

  increased presence in schools, 74

School-to-prison pipeline, 72, 73, 126, 128

  criminalize student behavior, 73

  starts in preschool, 128

Schott Black Boys Report, 79-84

  graduation rates for black males, 80, 81, 83

Schott Foundation, 79

Separate-and-unequal, v, 4, 9, 13, 15, 17, 188

Separate-but-equal, 45, 182

Shack, Francina, 180

Site assessment, 158

Situational leader, 157

Smith, Murray, 155

Social facilitation, 165
Spencer, Richard, 185
Sputnik, 52
   baby-boomer families, 52
   launching, 52
   "space race", 52
St. Paul's College (VA), 98
   forced to close due to lack of funding, 98
Statue of Liberty, 97, 99
   "tired, poor, and huddled masses", 99
Stereotypes, 67, 79-86
   by teachers, 82, 86
   negative for blacks, 67, 79, 86
Stone, Angie, 154
Student-athletes, 33, 34
Structured conversations, 160-163
   administrators, 160
   students, 162
   teachers, 161
Student debt, 102-105, 116, 117, 123
   black-white debt gap, 103, 104
   black-white employment gap, 105
   burdens to repay loans, 104
   529 Plans, 117
   financial literacy, 117
   for African American students, 103
   management, 116, 117
   proposed legislation, 116, 117
   total in the US, 123
Student Nonviolent Coordinating Committee, 49
Summer Enrichment Program, 156, 170
Suspensions for minority students, 72, 85, 127
Sweatt v. Painter (1950), 15, 21
Swinton, Dr. David A., 156

T

Taylor, Hattie, v
Taylor, Jim, 155, 156, 159
Taylor, Dr. Wandy, 63, 64
Teacher certification, 142
   four levels in GA, 142
Teacher Effectiveness, 54-56, 58, 76, 77, 82, 84, 86, 87, 107
   African American teachers, 58, 82, 84, 86, 87, 107
   disparities in preparedness, 55
   disparities in training, 55
   diversity gap, 55, 56
   highly qualified, 76, 77
   student engagement, 56, 59
   "teacher effect", 55
Teachers, 66, 146-150
   lack of respect for in USA, 146-150
   preparation programs, 66, 145
   the Boldens, 146
   national shortages, 142, 147
Teacher-Student racial gap, 139
Teacher Training Programs, 141-145
   knowledge of the subject, 141

how to teach the subject, 141
professional development, 143, 145
pre-service, 142, 145
in-service, 142, 145

Theismann, Joe, 36

The New Teacher Project, 150, 153
challenges for recruiting teachers, 153
eight strategies to retain teachers, 150

The Problem We Must All Live With (Rockwell), 19

Thomas, Clarence, 31, 42
his view regarding affirmative action, 31
received a college scholarship that was reserved for minority students, 31

Three R's, 2
reading, 'riting, 'rithmetic, 2
relief, recovery, and reform, 2

Tinker v. Des Moines (1969), 51
students' rights to free speech, 51

Title I, 67-72, 76, 85, 87, 134
highly-qualified teachers, 72, 76
low expectations, 71, 87
Matthew Effect, 71
schools, 85, 134
student achievement, 69-71

Trump, Donald, 65, 114, 189
fuels xenophobia, 65
views on public education, 189

U

Uncle Remus, 4, 6

Brer Bear, 4
Brer Fox, 4
Brer Rabbit, 4
The Wonderful Tar-Baby Story, 4

United Federation of Teachers, 50
provided teachers for Freedom Schools, 50

University of Alabama, 23
forced desegregation of, 23

University of Georgia, 21, 22
black students denied enrollment, 21

University of Mississippi, 22
violent response to integration, 22

University of South Carolina, vii, 31, 32, 184
admissions criteria, 32
wave of integration in 1966, 184

U.S. Department of Defense Dependent Schools (DoDDS), v

U.S. Department of Education, 63, 72, 115
Civil Rights & Data Collection, 72, 74, 75, 115
The State of Racial Diversity, 63

U.S. Supreme Court, 3, 4, 14-18, 21-28, 42, 131, 185
"all deliberate speed", 17
Plessy v Ferguson, 3, 23

W

Wallace, Gov. George, 23
"segregation forever", 23

Wallace, Rachell, 161

Washington, Booker T., 11-13, 46
   industrial education, 11
   Tuskegee Institute, 11, 46

Washington, Chad, 180

Why Teachers Can't Teach (Kline), 120

Wilbanks, J. Alvin, 74

William Frantz School, 18

Winfrey, Oprah, 43

Witty, Dr. Jan, 155, 172

Work Study Program, 37, 38

Z

Zero tolerance policies, 74, 76, 126, 127, 152
   increase in suspensions, 127, 152
   ineffective, 126, 152

Zimmerman, George, 78, 79

CPSIA information can be obtained
at www.ICGtesting.com
Printed in the USA
FFOW03n0715200318
45843202-46731FF